COAT OF MANY COLORS

20 INSPIRATIONAL STORIES TO INSPIRE AND AWAKEN THE "DREAMER" IN YOU TO FULFILL YOUR DREAMS!

COMPILED BY

KISHMA A. GEORGE

Contents

Publisher's Foreword

What a privilege and an honor for this book "Coat of Many Colors" to be the fourteenth book that ChosenButterfly Publishing has published in collaboration with Dr. Kishma A. George! Throughout the last decade of partnering on book releases with Dr. Kishma, the consistent underlying theme has been Dream and Dream Big. As a result of being a big dreamer herself, I have seen Dr. Kishma accomplish many great feats which solidifies that when you write the vision and do the work IT WILL COME TO PASS!

A key practice in Dr. Kishma's book collaborations involves inviting individuals to contribute their testimonies, sharing their diverse experiences and expertise. This approach serves to not only inspire dreams but also equip others to achieve their aspirations.

This book *Coat of Many Colors* is no exception. *Coat of Many Colors* is a powerful anthology of personal stories that showcases the triumph of the human spirit in the face of adversity. This book features 20 co-authors hand-picked by Dr. Kishma, who share their experiences of faith, favor, betrayal, and destiny. Each narrative is an intimate testament to the strength of ambitious dreaming and the unwavering pursuit of one's godly purpose. Some of these stories are raw, candid, and deeply personal, shedding light on the grueling yet transformative journeys undertaken by these remarkable individuals.

Using the biblical story of Joseph as a backdrop, readers are reminded when you have a God given dream and the favor of God on your life you have everything you need to rise above ALL setbacks, challenges and everything else that life throws your way. With God ALL things are possible, and YOU are more than a conquer.

Here at ChosenButterfly Publishing 'We Publish Books That Transforms Lives' and I believe this book you are holding *Coat of Many Colors* has the ability to do just that! Enjoy and be Empowered!

Love & Blessings,

www. Cb-publishing.com

Ayanna Lynnay

CEO and Founder ChosenButterfly Publishing

Wear Your Coat of Many Colors!!

Kishma A. George

One day, I sat on my bed and cried out to God. I was so sick and tired of my life situations. I told God there has to be more to life than this. My life was the same routine day by day, living from paycheck to paycheck, going to work, church and back home. In that season of my life, I was working at a fast food restaurant although I had a degree in psychology. Some of my college friends would come into the restaurant and see me mopping the floors and cleaning the toilets. They laughed at me and said it was a shame because I was not motivated to do better with myself. But deep down inside, I knew I would not be working in a restaurant for the rest of my life. I kept working at the restaurant until my working hours were cut to the on-call shift.

One day, I went to the grocery store using food stamps and I met a young lady who graduated from the same college I attended. She told me about her new job and then asked me the question I dreaded answering at that time of my life "Where do you work?" I answered that I am still employed but have no working hours at this time, but I'm sending out my resume and filling out job applications. Then she asked me what my degree was, and I told her psychology. She informed me that there was an agency hiring people for a Wraparound Therapist position. She said that this job position assist youths in the foster care system and I should apply. My reply to her was that I had no experience working with youths in the foster care system. She looked at me with a smile and said I can do anything I put my mind to do. I felt within myself that God was ordering my steps. She gave me the contact information and I faxed my resume the next day. A few days later, I received a phone call for a job interview for the job that works with youths in the foster care. I was so excited, and I prayed to God the night before the interview that He would give me the right words to say. The next day, I went to the job interview and got hired on the spot. God was teaching me that when situations look impossible in life, all things are possible with Him and that I should stand still and see the salvation of the Lord!

While working as a Wraparound Therapist, I witnessed the tremendous challenges the youths who aged out of the foster care experienced while trying to find their way to a self-sufficient and stable life. A passion within me grew for the aged-out youths and their future as I experienced their frustration in handling basic skills, such as opening a checking/savings account, parenting, and the frustration of single parents. Many of the youths with whom I worked with left foster care at 18 years old and found themselves homeless, pregnant, lacking self-esteem, incarcerated, unemployed, and without guidance. They struggled in their transition of leaving their foster homes because many were still attending high school and were not emotionally or financially stable. There was one story that really touched my heart; it was then I knew I wanted to make a difference in the lives of youths aging out of the foster care system and make certain that they had a safe, successful transition to adulthood and independent living. While working as an Independent Living Mentor, I mentored a young man who aged out of the foster care system. He had just turned 18yrs old, and I asked the foster mom if he can stay in her home for a while until I could find a place for him to live and a job. The foster mom told me that she will not receive a check for him staying at her home, so he will be able to stay there because of her income wages. We left her home that day, and I drove around Dover, Delaware, until 5:00 Pm looking for shelter openings. All the shelters were full. With tears in his eyes, he told me to drop him off at his brother's job, and he would sleep outside the restaurant that night. When I dropped him off, I told him that I would pick him up and I would make sure he got into a shelter for at least 30 days. As I drove home, I as saying to myself something had to be done for youths aging out of the foster care system. That night, I tossed and turned all night lying in my bed, thinking about the young man's safety. The next day, I picked up him and went straight to the Legislature Hall. A senator was able to get the young man in a shelter that day. As a mentor, it gave me 30 days to help the young man find employment and an apartment.

As I continued working with youths aging out of the foster care, the Lord laid in my heart to open a transitional home for youths aging out of the foster care system in Delaware. I laughed, God, really? I'm not business-minded, I'm very shy, I don't like speaking in front of people, God you know I failed speech class twice in college, I have no money, help, and resources, and the list went on and on. Several months went by, and the Lord spoke to me again to yield to the vision He gave me, to open a transitional home for young women who were aging out of the foster care system in Delaware. As I sat on the bed that night, I surrendered and yielded to God's plan.

I was very excited about the vision. My faith and confidence in God increased. I began saying I can do all things through Christ that strengthens me. I was very excited about the vision and told a friend of mine what the Lord instructed me to do, and her response was so negative. Her response was, *can you really open a transitional home without money or resources??* She said that I had never done it before, it will not work, and it was impossible. When I got off the phone, I was tired of all the negativity. I prayed to God to send positive friends in my life. Friends who would push me into my destiny!

I want to encourage you today that you have to be very careful who you share your dreams with! Remember what happened to Joseph in the bible; he shared his dream with his brothers, and they got angry and sold him. Not every person can comprehend who you are in God and what plans God has for your life. Surround yourself with positive people. People with Faith! People with Vision and Dreams! People who will inspire, empower, and motivate you and push you into your destiny! You have to guard your mind against dream killers and distance yourself from the small-minded and negative people who want to pull you down. Having positive relationships and the right people around you will empower you to reach your highest potential in God!

So, I encourage you today that when you have a dream, do not give up even if you lose money pursuing your dreams, if people walk out on you; if no one wants to fund your dreams, if there is a lack of support, etc. DREAM Again & DREAM BIG!!

Some of you reading this book, God showed you a vision that you will open a business, publish a book, write songs, teach, preach, open a shelter, write stage plays, open a non-profit, make-up line, clothing store, shoe store, a mini-mall, mentor, produce music, write poetry, etc., and you ask God, "Can it really happened?" God is saying, "Yes...if you only Believe! God wants to bring forth the Dreamer in YOU! Remember, with God all things are POSSIBLE! God wants us to Dream outside the box. **Eph. 3:20** states, "Now unto us who is able to do exceeding abundantly above all that we ask or think; according to the power that worketh in us." God's Word plainly and clearly states our purpose, which is to be God's hands on this earth. God wants you to succeed, and if you are willing to step up to the plate, you will not fail because God will never leave you nor forsake you.

To every dreamer reading this, I want to encourage you to DREAM AGAIN!! When you have a dream, walk by faith and not by sight. The belief that dreams are impossible to achieve stops people from getting what they really want. People are what they believe themselves to be. **Proverbs 23:7** says, "For as he thinketh in his heart, so is he!" If you want success, start thinking of yourself as a success. True success is the progressive achievement of your God-inspired goals. Success is the result of living in alignment with God's laws of success. God did not make you with limitations... **Mark 9:23** says, "All things are possible to him that believeth." Believe that new and exciting opportunities are coming your way in this NEW SEASON because God is not through blessing you! Whatever vision God has showed you, believe His Word and step out in faith until it is manifested in your life. It's time to wear your coat of many colors!!!

Dr. Kishma George Acknowledgements

First and foremost, I want to give God all the glory and honor as He made this vision possible. I love You, Lord, with all my heart! ♥ In memory of my beloved father, Edmond Felix George, I am thankful for his encouragement and inspiring me to dream. ♥To the best mother in the world, Novita Scatliffe-George, I thank you for your love, support, encouraging words, and praying for me. Thank you for not giving up on me. I love you, Mom! ♥To my wonderful daughter Kiniquá, I love you dearly. Thank you for your encouraging words, hugs and love. ♥ To my family, James, Raeisha, Christopher, Joshua, Seriah, Janisha, and Kayla — thank you for supporting the vision with your prayers and love. ♥♥A special thank you to the co-authors of the Coat of Many Colors Dr. Gail James, Prophetess Shirlene Jones, Minister Claudine Noel, Ambassador Cenena Lowe, Eliyah Shmuel Ben Yah, Keisha LeToy Glass, Prophetess Sylvia Castillo, Edwina Wilson, Dr. Jacquelyn Hadnot, Pastor Rodney Davis, Dr. Victoria Woods, Rashonda Henley, Pastor Frank Gibbs, Dr. Tamika Stanford Daniels, Dr. Sharon Simon, Dr. Tameka Stanford Daniels, Minister Kisha Battle Houston, Dr. Amicitia Maloon-Gibson, and Dr. Natasha Bibbins!!

A special thank you to my beautiful Jackie Hicks for her amazing photography, beautiful Letitia Thornhill for her gift of make-up artistry. Love you, ladies! ♥ To K.I.S.H. Home, Inc.'s board/advisors, volunteers, and mentors: thank you for your dedication, support, and for believing in the vision of helping make a difference in the lives of young women in Delaware. To Emily Ann Warren, thank you for your support, love, and for believing in me. To Pastor Ayanna, publisher: I thank God every day for bringing you into my life. You have been a blessing. Thank you for your encouraging words, support, love, and for believing in the vision. Love you. ♥Last but not least, I would like to thank ChosenButterfly Publishing and everyone who encouraged, prayed for, and supported K.I.S.H. Home, Inc. over the years; I am forever grateful. God Bless!

Dr. Kishma A. George

In a single phrase, Dr. Kishma A. George can be described as a Purpose Pusher. She is an inspirational speaker, prophetess, entrepreneur, mentor, playwright, tv host, radio personality, producer, and best-seller author, and her overarching mission is to inspire people to fulfill their God-given purpose. Dr. Kishma's work as a speaker and mentor is executed through the Women Destined for Greatness Mentoring Program in Kent County, DE. She believes that despite life's circumstances, there is greatness inside of you!

Dr. Kishma A. George is the President and CEO of K.I.S.H. Home, Inc., acronym for Kingdom Investments in Single Hearts (K.I.S.H.) K.I.S.H. Home Inc. was founded out of a desire to positively impact the lives of girls and women in the state of Delaware. Dr. Kishma A. George is the President and CEO of K.I.S.H. (Kingdom Investments in Single Hearts) Home, Inc. K.I.S.H. Home, Inc. was founded out of the desire to make an impact in the lives of girls and women in Delaware, as well as those young women who are presently in or have aged out of the foster care system.

Dr. George worked as an Independent Living Mentor and witnessed the tremendous challenges aged-out foster care youth experienced while trying to find their way to a self-sufficient and stable life. A passion within her grew for these young adults and their future as she experienced their frustration in handling basic skills, such as opening a checking/savings account, parenting, and the frustration of single parenthood.

Dr. George knew that these young adults, whether they were a single-parent or single, needed a strong support system that would empower and encourage them to take control of their lives. They struggled in their transition of leaving foster care because many were still attending high school and were not emotionally or financially stable. After witnessing this, Dr. George began her journey of seeking ways to assist young adults in becoming emotionally and economically self-sufficient so that their transition out of the foster care system and into independent living was successful. Many of the young adults with whom she worked with, left the foster care system at 18 years old and found themselves homeless, pregnant, lacking self-esteem, incarcerated, unemployed, and without guidance. As a mentor, Dr. George became frustrated by the minimum amount of resources the community offered these young adults.

Dr. Kishma's dream came to pass, and she opened a 24-hour transitional home for young women presently in or have aged out of the foster care system in Delaware. She makes a difference in their lives and makes certain that they have a safe, successful transition to adulthood and independent living.

Her diligence and passion for young women have been recognized in various newspaper articles, including the Dover Post, Delaware News Journal, Delaware State News, and Milford Beacon. She was also featured in the Wisdom for Everyday Life, Kingdom Voices Magazine, Gospel 4 U Magazine, K.I.S.H. Magazine, BOND Inc., and BlogSpot's week spotlight "Fostered Out of Love." In addition she has appeared as a special guest on the Atlanta LIVE TV Show, Delmarva WBOC- ABC, Life Talk Radio Show with Coach TMB, Live TV Show Straight Talk for Women Only, 101.7 FM Radio, FoxFire Radio Show and The Frank and Travis Radio Show on Praise 105.1. Empowered Women Ministries have recognized Dr. Kishma as

Woman of the Year in the category of Entrepreneurial Success, as well as Zeta Phi Beta Sorority, Inc./ Theta Zeta Zeta Chapter for her outstanding involvement in the Greater Dover Community. She was also presented with the Diversity Award (2013) from the State of Delaware/Social Services, the Authentic Servant Leadership Award (2014) & New Castle County Chapter of the DSU Alumni Association 33rd annual Scholarship Luncheon for outstanding service to the Wilmington Community and the Delaware State University (2014), Church Girlz Rock; Humanitarian Award (2015), Faith Fighter Award (2016), CHOICES "Woman of the Year"(2016), State of Delaware Office of the Governor Tribute Award (2016), Business Woman of the Year (2016), Global Smashers Award (2017), I AM Baby Doll Global Award (2018), I AM Entrepreneurship Devorah Award (2018) Business Woman of the Year Award (2018) World-Changer Award (2019), I Am Fabulous Award (2019), Phenomenal Woman of the Year (2019), Mogul of the Month (2020). Woman of Influence Spotlight (2020), Phenomenal Woman of the Year (2022), and International Business Award (2023).

Contacts Information:

FB- @kishmageorge
Clubhouse- @kishmageorge
IG-@drkishmageorge
Twitter-@kishmageorge
TickTok -@kishmageorge
Website: www.kishmageorge.com

The Coat

Frank W. Gibbs, JR.

coat can be defined as a garment worn outdoors. To most, it is a protective layer or covering to shield the elements. Coats vary in length and style according to fashion and use. Regardless of how fashionable they may appear, the purpose of a coat is to provide an extra layer of protection from the elements. Joseph was gifted a coat of many colors by his father. However, his coat didn't necessarily provide him with protection from some of the things he would encounter in his life's journey. As a matter of fact, his coat caused him to be envied, despised and rejected by his family, particularly his brothers. The Bible informs us that his father loved him more than all his other children and when his brothers saw this, the Bible says they hated or envied him. Joseph didn't silicate or beg his father for the coat; his father freely gave it to him. To reiterate, it was a gift from his father that represented favor. The favor in your life is a gift from your Heavenly Father. You didn't silicate him for it; it was given to you freely because of his love for you. God loves us so much that he will give us unique blessings that are tailor-made just for us. That's why it's not wise to be jealous of anyone else's blessing(s) because what God has for you is tailor-made just for you. You don't have to compete, compare, or be intimidated by anyone else. What God has for you, is for you. Notice Joseph didn't have to compete or contend with his brothers for the coat his father gave him because what the father had for him was made specifically for him. As with Joseph, what the father has for you is specifically for you. When God gives you his favor, no one can take it from you.

The coat that his father gave him was an outward symbol of favor. Joseph's brothers would later take his coat from him, but the favor of God was still on his life. God's favor is not limited to what's on you; his favor goes far beyond that. In other words, God's favor is not just limited to material possessions. Material possessions may be a byproduct of his favor, but you can have his favor without materialism. This is what confuses many people. They see others with nice homes, vehicles, etc., and assume that this is all favor consists of. However, you can live without many of those things and still have God's favor upon your life. God's favor is the ability to take you places that you could not ordinarily go on your own. Joseph lost the coat his father gave him, but he still became a mighty leader in Egypt. So, even though the outward symbol of favor was no longer with him, he still carried the favor of God wherever he went. Think about it: this young man had no type of political experience, yet he was placed in one of the most prominent leadership positions in the world at that time. The favor of God upon his life enabled him to save entire generations of people all over the world. That's what favor does; it takes you places that you could not ordinarily go on your own. God's favor will put you in places where your resume or job experience doesn't qualify you to go. The favor of God on your life will take you further than you could ever imagine. The scripture informs us in *Ephesians 3:20 "Now unto him that is able to do exceeding abundantly above all that we ask or think, according to the power that worketh in us, (KJV)."* Our biggest, most outlandish goal, dream, or prayer request in life, God wants us to know that he can go above and beyond anything for that. Favor goes above and beyond anything that we may ask or think. Joseph knew that one day, he would be in a position of leadership. However, he probably never imagined that his leadership role would be as impactful as it was and that centuries later, his name would still be mentioned as one of the great heroes of faith. I've gotten into a practice that whenever I'm asked to perform a task or when I'm about to go to a place I've never been before to speak, preach, etc., one of the first things I do when I get there is say "Lord, thank you for your favor." I'm literally making a declaration over my life that where I am is because of God's favor. And I take solace in knowing that God has already given me the knowledge, strength and help that I need to accomplish the task at hand. Every time we tell God, "Lord, thank you for your favor," we are releasing his favor upon our lives. So, I would encourage you to make a declaration over your life at the beginning of every day that you have God's favor. The Bible says in *Proverbs 18:21 "Death and life are in the power of the tongue: and they that love it shall eat the fruit thereof, (KJV)."* You have been given the authority to release God's favor in your life. You don't have to wait for someone else to release it; you have the power to release it upon yourself. Favor is with you, on you, in you and around you, and remember, no one can remove it once the Lord has released it to you. You will be mighty in the land; you will establish a legacy that will live on even after you are gone. Your family will be prosperous because of God's favor on your life. Don't shortchange yourself, you are unique and one of a kind, and God has you here for such a time as this so that you can make an impact on the entire world. That's what happened to Joseph; he made an impact on the entire world with no experience and no formal training; all he had was the favor of God. When you realize that the favor of God is all you have, you realize that the favor of God is all you need. Joseph didn't have many people supporting him. His family wasn't in his corner; Potiphar's wife accused him of a crime he did not commit, which resulted in him having to serve out a prison sentence. While in prison, his so-called friends abandoned him and forgot all about him until it was time for him to interpret a dream for the king. So, when you have been given favor don't expect everyone to be supportive. Don't expect everyone to encourage you or motivate you. Most of the time, great leaders are people who must walk alone. Most leaders are secluded and isolated, with very little to no friends. If you are feeling alone, like no one is there for you when you need them the most, you are in good company. Every leader in Biblical history had moments of isolation, rejection and seclusion. That's just how it is, but to reiterate, if you have God's favor with you, that's all you need.

Everywhere Joseph went he was successful because God was with him. Life is a journey and none of us will know what will occur during the journey, but if God is with us, we can rest assured that wherever we may end up in this journey that we will be guaranteed complete success. Joseph knew that one day, he would become a powerful leader. What he did not know was what would take place prior to him becoming a powerful leader. He had no idea the type of suffering that he would have to endure for him to become great. There are some things that God will reveal to us concerning our future. However, there are certain things that God will purposely conceal from us because he understands that it could discourage us from pursuing the dream that he has for us. The act of suffering or being tested is the least appealing aspect of Christianity. Although it may be the least appealing, it is the most beneficial aspect of our Christian journey. For us to evolve into the individuals that God has predestined for us to be, we have to be tested and we will face adversity *1 Peter 4:1 "Forasmuch then as Christ hath suffered for us in the flesh arm yourselves likewise with the same mind: KJV."* Jesus is our prime example. He was the leader of leaders. He was a man of purpose and destiny. Yet even though he was a man of purpose and destiny, and the greatest leader the world has ever known, he still had to deal with adversity and suffering. So, the question is, if Jesus, our Lord and Savior, had to deal with his share of adversity on his way to fulfilling his assignment here on earth, what makes us assume that we won't have to? The greater the adversity, the greater the purpose. The Bible says in *2 Corinthians 4:7 "But we have this treasure in earthen vessels that the excellency of the power may be of God and not us."* Treasure is something that is considered extremely valuable and priceless.

It cannot be found anywhere, it's something that's normally hidden and out of plain view. All of us have a treasure hidden deep within us. What you have is priceless, it's unique, it's exceptional, and it's valuable. People like you come once in a lifetime. There will never be another you. You have been called into the kingdom for such a time as this. That's why the enemy comes against you. That's why he fights relentlessly, attempting to make you give up because he knows that you are a dreamer who will change the entire world. Don't allow where you are today and what you are going through to discourage you from where you will be tomorrow. Trouble comes to all of us, particularly those of us who are destined for greatness. The good news about trouble is that trouble has an expiration date. Eventually, the trouble will pass and you will become who God has called you to be; *2 Corinthians 4:17 "For our light affliction, which is but for a moment, worker for us a far more exceeding and eternal weight of glory, (KJV)."* Notice the Bible describes them as being light. They may seem heavy to us, but the Bible says they are light, and then it says it's only for a moment. A moment is something that comes and goes. It doesn't last long. The enemy would love for us to focus more on the light affliction of the moment than what's coming after the moment. According to the word of God, the glory that comes after the affliction is going to be greater. You must constantly remind yourself that God has something greater for you. As a matter of fact, that should be your daily declaration that where I am, I will not always be. A greater blessing is coming to me; greater doors are opening for me, and great opportunities are going to be presented to me. Never get caught up in the now because the now will eventually change.

Joseph had to stay committed to his dream. He had to look beyond what was in front of him and see his future. He knew that God had made him a promise. He knew that he would eventually become a great leader, but he had to remain consistent and committed. Commitment and consistency always pay off in the end. Many people have dreams and ambitions but lack the commitment and consistency to accomplish them. The Lord wants you to stay committed and consistent. Dr. Myles Monroe made one of the most prolific and thought-provoking statements I've ever heard. He said on one occasion, "The wealthiest place on the planet is the grave." He went on to say that there are songs that have never been sung in the grave. Some of the greatest poetry that we've never read is in the grave. Some of the greatest inventions, actors, singers, musicians that would have made an impact on history are lying in the grave. The cure for some of the world's deadliest diseases is lying in the grave. It is my sincere conviction that the reason they are lying in the grave is because most of the people that possessed these dreams gave up on them. Perhaps when they shared their dreams of one day changing the world they were met with hostility. Perhaps when they shared their ideas of wanting to do something great, they were ridiculed, mocked and felt ashamed. Some of them may have encountered odious remarks and they decided to give up. Whatever the reason may be, many people gave up prematurely and never accomplished their dreams. However, that will not be said about you. You are not going to give up. You will accomplish whatever it is that God has designed for you. Pressure comes at all of us. Life can be cruel; the people around us can be cruel. But don't let that stop you from being committed to your dream.

Every one of us will have things that will come against us. People will come against us. Our adversary, the devil, will come against us. However, God placed something that is so great and powerful within us that regardless of what we may face, we will overcome because *1 John 4:4 "Greater is he that is in us, than he that is in the world, (KJV)."* What God placed within you is an investment in his kingdom and this world, and God will take care of his investment. God is going to take care of you like he did to Joseph. Yes, Joseph was tested and tried, but God took care of him through it all. God protected him, provided for him, and was with him, and everything he encountered in his life was only building his character to make him a great leader.

Trials strengthen your character. Without them, you could never become a great leader. When God puts you in a position of leadership, he will make sure that you have been tested and tried because the last thing that God wants to do is to place an individual into leadership prematurely. When Joseph arrived in Egypt as a ruler and 2nd in command to Pharoah, he was prepared. He didn't lack anything. He had mental fortitude; he had wisdom and he had authority. If he didn't go through what he went through, he would have never been able to be an effective leader. Leadership comes with a price. But it's worth the wait when you finally reach the place where God has intended for you to be. You don't have to rush, you're not in competition with anyone else; when it's your time, it is your time. God knows when to release you and he knows when you are ready. We must learn to wait on the Lord and allow him to shape and mold us. I used to get frustrated when I felt as though God wasn't moving fast enough for me. I would be angry with God. My frustration almost led to my personal and spiritual demise. One day, as I was airing my grievances to God, he spoke to me and said, "According to my time, it will happen." When he spoke that into my spirit, a spirit of calmness and tranquility immediately came upon me. From that point, I realized I'm not sure when God would do it, but I know he promised me that he will do it, and that's all I need. I don't need to know all the details, the when, the why, the what and the where. All I needed to know was that God told me he's going to do it and that was enough for me. Maybe you are like I was–frustrated, angry, confused, etc. God says it's coming. If it didn't come today, that means, it's a possibility it's coming tomorrow. If it doesn't come tomorrow, that means it could come the day after tomorrow but everyday you're inching closer and closer to your promise. Don't allow the enemy to make you feel like you've missed your opportunity. It's closer than you think. I can remember another time I needed clarity from God. As I was driving, he told me to read the caption on my side mirror of the vehicle. I said God, this doesn't make sense. He told me again, read the caption on your side mirror. So, I did what he told me to do. The caption on your side mirror says, "Objects in mirror are closer than they appear." God spoke to me and told me what I have been praying for is closer than it appears. It may seem like it's far away, but it's closer than you think. What God has in store for you is closer than it appears.

Joseph had a coat that he eventually lost. The coat was a symbol of favor. He may have lost his coat, but he never lost his favor. Regardless of what you may have lost over the years, the Lord wants to remind you that this favor is still upon your life. And his favor will remain upon your life until your earthly assignment is completed. Don't be discouraged by what you may have lost in life. What God is about to give you will make up for every loss you've encountered in your entire life. Don't stop dreaming, don't stop believing, don't stop chasing after your dreams because sooner than later, you're going to be everything that God has called you to be.

Frank W. Gibbs, JR. Acknowledgements

There are a few people that have made this book eminently more readable than it otherwise might have been. The first being my wife, Lisa. Lisa, you have been a reliable source in my life since we've been married. We've had our share of ups and downs, storms and rain, etc., but through it all, we've managed to stay together with the help of the Lord. I'm a better person because of you, and I'm grateful for you. My daughter Kyela for caring enough about me to tell me the truth even when I don't want to hear it. My father, Frank Gibbs, SR. You've shown me how to be a man. Because of you, I realized that for anything you want in this life, you must go after and not sit there and wait for anything to just fall out of the sky. I would also like to thank my church family for believing in me and encouraging me to continue to press forward. Lastly, I would like to thank my Pastor, Bishop Jesse Abbott. Thank you for being my Prophet Samuel. As with David, I was content tending to my daily tasks when you approached me and told me that God was transitioning me from tending to sheep to becoming a king. Your gracious support has enabled me to evolve into what God has predestined for me to be.

Frank W. Gibbs, JR.

Frank W. Gibbs, JR. is a native of the Delaware Eastern Shore. He leverages his pioneering vision and instinct to serve others in areas extending beyond the church. Frank Gibbs is a motivational speaker, pastor, playwright, radio personality, poet, husband and friend. However, his greatest attribute is his ability to serve others. For over 20 years, Pastor Gibbs has inspired many with his messages of hope and restoration. Although he was reared in an extremely strict Pentecostal home, he was able to widen his spiritual parameters to reach people of all backgrounds and cultures. His ministry promotes spiritual and self-awareness, empowerment, and encouragement through sound Biblical teaching. He is charismatic yet remains humble. His impact on evangelism and outreach is unparalleled. He is the CEO and founder of G-Thang Entertainment, enabling him to launch several successful gospel plays/productions that have drawn crowds of thousands of people from all over the East Coast.

Gibbs began his ministry at the tender age of 19, when he was ordained as minister. As time progressed, his ministry continued to progress, which made him a much sought-after speaker in the years to come. He has a true heart for evangelism and loves to do outreach in his local community. His motto is "When the church goes into the community, the community will go into the church." Pastor Gibbs believes that evangelism is the heartbeat of any ministry. He and his parishioners have initiated several outreach programs in their local community, such as free food giveaways, toy drives for marginalized children, scholarships, etc.

In 2015, he transitioned into the role of assistant pastor for New Dimensions Family Ministries in Salisbury, MD. A year later, he was appointed as the campus pastor of the New Dimensions Millsboro Campus, located in Millsboro, DE. He is constantly emerging as a premier leader in the areas of ministry, outreach and media. On September 4, 1999, he was joined in holy matrimony to his wife, Lisa A. Gibbs. From this union, they have one daughter, Kyela Gibbs, and he's been blessed with two bonus sons, Tobias Loper and Jaron Dukes.

Joseph And The Family Fire Tests / God's Redemptive Plan

Dr. Tamike Brown

The Joseph story is known to many people around the world although there are some who may have never heard of it. It is found in the book of Genesis and details the story of family betrayal that started because of favor and a dream. Your story or my story may not have been exactly like Joseph's story, but I can sure tell you that my story has and had many similarities to Joseph's story because I, too, was a victim of the family fire tests. And just like Joseph at the time, he probably didn't know why or even understood so much of the family fire tests, but in the end, you will learn that he was part of "God's Redemptive Plan."

It is very important for me to write this story because, as I mentioned, my story is somewhat similar to Joseph's story. I can write my story, tell my story, or even preach my story, but today, I choose to write a little bit about Joseph's story, which will be an introduction to my true story to be released in a book called Birth Out Of The Fire Volume 2.

It is in my heart's desire to so much so to write this story that if I didn't write it, it would prolong my healing towards reaching my destiny. Sometimes, an individual can think or believe he or she is healed from past hurt and pain, especially from family members until the same routine pattern continues to go on and on from the same people that brought the initial pains. When

I write, it releases me so I can release them. You know the story, it's called "forgive" for real so I can be healed! I wasn't healed for real because there still was a sore spot in the deal.

I don't share my story to shame anyone or for anyone to be looked down upon, I share my story of the family fire tests so I can be set free to do the Will of God for my life because my Heavenly Father has need of me. Dr. Maya Angelou once said, "There is no greater agony than bearing an untold story inside of you." Writing my story sets me free! No matter the outcome of how one may view me or think of me, I will use the strategy God has given me to set me free from the pain of agony that I was carrying on the inside of me. The Love Strategy! The Root to the Fruits!

During Joseph's time, we hear about the Coat of Many Colors. And the Coat of Many Colors signifies Divine Love, Favor, Honor, and Destiny, which still holds true today. A person of Distinction!

At the age of 17, Joseph was working in the fields with his brothers. His brothers were doing things they shouldn't be doing, so he reported it to his father. Of course, the brothers were angry with him and considered him to be a tale-a-tell sort of speaker. Joseph's belief in obedience didn't fit in with his brothers' behavior of disobedient and evil mindsets, so he reported what he saw his brothers doing. Joseph believed in obeying his parents and God even if it would cost him his life.

Israel (Jacob), the father, loved Joseph more than any of his sons because he was the son of his old age, and he made him a coat of many colors. When the other brothers saw that Jacob loved him more than all of them, they hated him. Then, one day, Joseph had a dream and decided to share it with his brothers out of excitement, not completely understanding the dream at the time in its fullness, but was excited to share it with his family. When he shared the dream with his brothers, instead of them liking him, they hated him even more. They became jealous and envious of him. *Be very careful who you share your dreams with, including family members and friends, because those who used to like you will begin to turn against you.* The interesting thing about his sharing the dreams with his family is that they knew exactly what the dreams meant, even if Joseph himself didn't know what it meant in totality.

One day, his father sent Joseph out of obedience to go check on his brothers who were working in the field. His brothers saw Joseph coming from a distance and immediately, they plotted to kill him because they were jealous of him because he was their father's favorite son, and the youngest next to baby Benjamin. They saw him coming and said let's kill the dreamer and throw him into the pit. They wanted to kill the dreamer because they were afraid the dreams would come true. *They failed to realize you can't kill a dream that was meant to live. God ordained the dreams.* Because not only *did his father favor Joseph, he was chosen and favored by God too!*

One of the brothers said let us not kill him. Shed no blood! Throw him in the pit instead. His plan was to rescue Joseph, but that wasn't God's plan for him to rescue him. God chose Joseph, and when you are chosen by God, He allows you to go through the firer because He's getting ready to birth Himself through you. *They had a plan to kill him, but God had a plan to build him. Joseph was part of God's Redemptive Plan to help save God's people from starvation. He was the Financial Reservoir and A Ruler over the Agriculture Industry.* So when Joseph arrived on the scene, they immediately stripped him of his Coat of Many Colors and threw him in a dry pit and shortly sold by his brothers as a slave to the Ishmaelites.

The "coat of many colors" is probably one of the most known facts about Joseph, the son of Jacob. Jacob considered Joseph to be a gift from God in his old age. He gave him a coat as a special way of showing his love for his son. A coat with many colors, which is a Coat of Distinction. It says something about the person wearing it. A Coat of Honor. The Coat symbolizes the outworking of God's plan for Joseph. Joseph was special. God had big plans for Joseph. He would be the Heir to the family inheritance. I'll dive a little deeper into the story to point out some major points of Joseph life.

His brothers hated that he was especially loved. They hated that his father cared so much about him. When Joseph came their way in his fancy coat of many colors, their blood began to boil. They became very angry. Deep down, the brothers knew that there was something special about Joseph, and he had a bright future ahead with his God-given dreams that enraged them even more. The dreams were a validation of the coat of many colors. Therefore, whatever is going to happen to Joseph was ordained by God.

Joseph did not share these dreams with his brothers to rub them in their faces. He did not share these dreams with his brothers as a way of being arrogant. He wasn't boasting. He was excited about being a part of God's redemptive plan. He shared the dreams with his brothers out of love, thinking they would be excited with him, but instead, they hated him even more. They couldn't stand the idea of them bowing to him or him ruling over them.

Joseph had another dream, and he shared it again with them and his father. Israel rebuked him, but he kept the saying in his mind. And he probably rebuked him openly in front of his brothers because he knew how his brothers felt about Joseph and did not want his brothers to kill him. I believe he was trying to keep peace amongst the brothers.

The coat and the dreams tell us everything that's going to happen to Joseph has been ordained by God and it is a story of God's Divine Choice for a future deliverer or redeemer. Joseph is set for a divine destiny specially chosen for God's purpose. The coat is given, and then the coat is taken away from him by his brothers. His brothers were evil and wicked. They did evil things behind their father's back. Their hatred for Joseph had grown so out of control until they wouldn't even speak to him. They hated him because Joseph was not only favored by his father, but he was favored and loved by God too! So, they plotted to kill him!

Israel sent Joseph to check on his brothers. *"His brothers had gone off to Shechem where they were pasturing their father's flocks. Israel said to Joseph, "Your brothers are with flocks in Shechem. Come, I want to send you to them." Joseph said, "I'm ready." He said, "Go and see how your brothers and the flocks are doing and bring me back a report." He sent him off from the valley of Hebron to Shechem. **Genes 37: 12-14".***

Joseph learned his brothers weren't in Shechem. They didn't obey their father's instruction, instead they had gone on to some other place. *Disobedient and stiff neck rebels is what Moses would have probably called them.* So, they went all the way to Dothan to be far away from their father to do their dirty work against their brother Joseph because they knew Joseph would be sent to check on them at some point. So, the plot to kill him from a distance was planned on purpose.

Sure enough, here comes Joseph, the dreamer in his Coat of Many Colors and all his tassels, etc. They saw a man of great honor coming, and they said we must kill that dreamer and who will honor him then they thought. They were ragging mad; they couldn't stand the sight of seeing him coming. *Can you imagine the look his brothers had on their faces, rolling their eyes in the back of their head, turning up their noses, saying here he comes? Who does he think he is? You young rookie! He's not going to tell us what to do! He's not our daddy. He's not our Supervisor, and he's surely not going to be ruling over us because he's a dead boy!*

Here Joseph come with a smile on his face, ready to greet his brothers with love and joy, not knowing he was walking into a death plot planned by his brothers! The brothers' motivation was evil. They stripped him of his Coat. The Coat of Honor, which was a symbol of Divine Love and Destiny. Threw him into the pit and left to die. A pit back then was shaped like a coca cola bottle narrowed at the top but wide at the bottom. Basically, once you are in, there is no way out unless someone helps you out. After they threw him in the pit, they just knew he would be left for dead. They all sat down to eat as though nothing happened, saying we got rid of our problem. They saw him as a problem and not a blessing. Joseph was calling for help from the pit, crying in agony *(the inner and outer cry)*, saying help me, my brothers, don't do this to me. That meant nothing to his brothers. They continue to eat. They had no remorse at all. Only one of the brothers, Reuben, had empathy for him.

The brothers saw the Ishmaelites coming and decided to sell him to the Ishmaelites to gain a profit from the sale of their brother, who they wanted dead. They lied to Reuben. They dipped the coat in goat blood to return to their father so Israel (Jacob) would think a goat killed Joseph. Evil, wicked brothers! The Family Fire Tests! The coat of many colors is now stained with blood, a coat of blood.

To fast forward, Joseph isn't dead; Joseph became the second ruler in charge next to Potiphar. His brothers bowed down to him there, not knowing they were bowing to their brother Joseph. Joseph says to them. Look up! I AM YOUR BROTHER JOSEPH! They became afraid. Joseph cried so loud until everyone probably heard him. A cry from the pain of agony of the evil things that were done to him by his brothers. He still had a sore spot from the situation, so he had to release them by crying it out. In other words, he was forgiving them. And on the flip side of things, there was a cry of gladness as he was excited to see and connect with his family again. A family he thought he would never see again. God had a plan! The Family Fire Tests!

Joseph told them not to be afraid. What you meant for evil, God turned it around for the good. He stated God planned it that way! It was a setup by God. I am Joseph, Your Brother! The Rejected Deliverer of God's Divine Redemptive Plan to help save you from the "Death of Starvation"! Their lives are now in his hands, but instead of him killing them, he forgave them and decided to deliver them because it was a part of God's Redemptive Plan. The family fire tests! I Am Joseph!

Why do I share that story? Many people in the world today may have had a story similar to Joseph's where you were favored by your parents and the other siblings hated or disliked you because you were favored and chosen by God too! And when you have been chosen by God to do a great work, many times, God will use the ones that are close to you to shape, mold, and build you. Basically, He allows the fire tests to happen because He has a great plan for your life. You're being purified in the fire so you can come out looking like your Daddy, Our Father, which hath Heaven. You're carrying His Glory and He wants to birth Himself through you.

To be continued! Birth Out Of The Fire! Volume 2

Dr. Tamike Brown

Dr. Tamike Brown is a World Class Speaker, and Self-Motivated Driven Leader who is passionate in her purpose in helping individuals to discover their gifts and dominate in their area of giftings. She is a true influential, energetic trailblazer in her field with over 23 years of experience in leadership, public speaking, motivating, encouraging, counseling, coaching, educating, training, and more. She considers herself to be impactful in her position because she loves and enjoys what she does.

She is the Chief Operating Officer of Tamike Brown Ministries, Discover You With Tamike LLC, Outreach International Foundation Inc., GAFV TV Network, Salvation With Fire® Radio and Television Broadcast of Atlanta, Georgia.

An expert in her field, Dr. Tamike Brown is a *Neuroencoding Elite Licensed Specialist, Master Mind Brain Speaker and Coach, a Member of The National Speakers Association, a Member of Black Speakers Network, and a Member of The National Small Business Association (NSBA) Leadership council.* She holds a bachelor's degree in Business Management with an emphasis in accounting from DeVry University. A degree in Information and Office Technology from Central Georgia Technical College, and has received her Honorary Doctorate in Ecclesiastes Ministries.

Dr. Tamike Brown received The Presidential LifeTime Achievement Award in 2022. She received Top World Class Speaker of the Year Award 2023 with IAOTP. And has been included in Marquis Who's Who in America Biography, and Who's Who of Professional Women.

She is the author and publisher of "Birth Out Of The Fire: Living Life On The Run" Volume 1, which allowed her to discover her own gifts in the communication industry, as well as co-author of several other anthologies highlighting Her Story "From Oak Ave to Joe Wright Drive Headed to the Promised Land."

Her area of focus is to fulfill the will of God for her life in bringing souls into the Kingdom of God through ministry, business, or in whatever avenue is deemed necessary by seeking the Father's face on a daily basis to receive the blueprint and the strategies that will allow her to stay on the path that will lead to her Destiny.

In addition to the love and passion she has for the people, she considers herself to be impactful in her position because she loves and enjoys what she does, and she tries to pass that energy on to others so they too can enjoy and love what they have been called to do in making a difference in this world for the Kingdom of God by dominating in their area of giftings.

Websites:

https://tamikebrownministries.com/
http://www.dywtamikebrown.com/
https://outreachintfound.com/
https://gafvntv.org/watch-live-tv

Email:

Tamike.brown.ministrie@gmail.com
discoveryouwithtamike@gmail.com
outreach.int.foundation@gmail.com
gafv.network@gmail.com

In the Midst of Purpose

Rashonda Henley

What is purpose? I would like to define purpose as your reason for being. It's the reason for which you were created and exist. God's intention is clear; we're the ones who have to discover what it is by seeking Him and eating His word. The ultimate joy God found in creating and forming you and me was with His agenda in mind, just as it was for Joseph. When we take a look at the coat of many colors that Jacob gave to his son Joseph, it represented not only favor but also Joseph's destination. I honestly believe Jacob's love for his son Joseph, and the favor Joseph found with Jacob was symbolic of the favor Joseph found with God. Jacob had no clue at the time that the coat he made for his son was a divine move of God. This coat made a bold statement about Joseph's destiny and the purpose he was to fulfill on earth.

> *"When he told his father as well as his brothers, his father rebuked him and said, what is this dream you had? Will your mother and I and your brothers actually come and bow down to the ground before you?"* – **Genesis 37:10**

There are times in our lives when the dreams God gives us seem to amaze us. We may often look at ourselves, then look at the dream and ask, "How am I going to do that?" or the magnitude of it may leave us in awe! I often reflect on the dreams and visions God has given me, where I've fought just to hold onto the promise. Some days, my mental capacity felt like I couldn't

35

hold on much longer. But God reminded me that everything He will do through me has nothing to do with me. Therefore, if we consider Joseph for a moment and the tests he had to endure, we can see that he was being equipped to deliver a nation out of Egypt. He wisely rationed the country's produce in preparation for a time of famine. Who would have known that, just like Joseph, you would reign out of your bondage? I want to leave you with a few words: No matter what you see on the other side, God is going to see you through. Some may ask themselves, "What makes him/her so special? What's so unique about you that God would choose you to face such challenges and tests as Joseph did?" The answer is the favor of God! You must understand that authentic leadership is forged in the crucible. This is where you and I are pressed, hammered, and formed. The forging process eliminates any false copies of you because your suffering qualifies you to reign in places where your imposter cannot.

Therefore, Satan's chief work is to imitate the things of God and lead people astray through them. Satan is not a creator; he is an imitator. So, if the enemy tries to imitate Christ, surely, he will try to imitate you or cause you to walk in a false perception of who you really are and hinder you from fulfilling your full potential. The process of developing maturity to walk in purpose involves hardship, difficulty, disappointment, rejection, and much more. God never promised an easy road, but He promised to see us through whatever we face.

There are many ways to interpret the promise released upon Joseph's life. Whenever God speaks to us through dreams, prophecies, or any other means, we must remember that His purpose is to get our attention. I believe God was speaking to Joseph's destiny even in the womb, and He used Jacob to demonstrate the favor bestowed upon Joseph's life, not only from a natural perspective but from a divine standpoint. There is no other reason for God creating you except for His perfect and divine will.

One of the traps many believers and non-believers fall into, as I am also guilty of at times, is living for ourselves. At some point in our lives, we should ask ourselves if our dependency is solely on God. Are we willing to give up everything to take on the name of Christ? Are we willing to forgive and forget so we can move forward and obtain all that God has in store for us? Is indulging in the things that bring us pleasure worth it? Often, we get caught up in the cares of life, trying to figure out how things will be done. We may long for marriage or be distracted by our financial situation, employment, children, and various other worldly concerns that suffocate our purpose for being here.

When your purpose begins to suffocate beneath the perils of life, asphyxiation occurs, making it difficult to have a clear view of your target and goal. Have you ever tried to pursue something God put in your heart, only to face challenges and struggles that threatened to veer you off course from your purpose? That is why it is crucial to be mindful of who you are and to whom you belong. The word of God reminds us daily of our identity and our royal position in the kingdom of God. There is nothing you need that God hasn't already provided for you. Often, we lose sight of the value of time, energy, purpose, destiny, and even God Himself. The word of God instructs us not to worry about tomorrow, for each day has enough trouble of its own. Instead, seek first the kingdom of God. In the scriptures, we find antidotes to the issues that trouble us, offering solace and guidance for life's challenges.

As I sit here in my living room, deep in thought and meditation, I find myself pondering the significance of the coat of many colors. This coat was not just an ordinary garment; its beauty and meaning ruffled many feathers among Joseph's brothers. While it symbolized the favor upon Joseph's life, it became an object of envy for his siblings. As I visualize myself in Joseph's stead, I contemplate the betrayal he endured from his own blood brothers, who sold him into slavery and even contemplated taking his life to derail his purpose.

When we consider Joseph's position of favor, juxtaposed with the hardships he faced, it becomes apparent that his trajectory did not align with what many would perceive as favorable. People often judge based on one's current status or the challenges of their past, throwing unexpected curveballs to divert their path and then spreading rumors as if they had sinned. When we think about great favor, the process of obtaining it is seldom discussed; the suffering one may have endured or would have to endure is often unspoken of.

We often focus on Joseph's dreams, which hold significant meaning on their own. However, amidst the purpose and promising dreams, there was a young man who suffered physical, mental, and emotional agony. If we take a moment to imagine Joseph's physical, mental, and emotional state, it doesn't paint a pleasant picture. Betrayed by his own brothers, sold into slavery, spending years in prison for refusing to engage in sin, forgotten by those he had helped—there are moments in our own lives where our suffering seems unbearable, and it appears as though the enemy will prevail.

Who could have known that Joseph's dreams would bring him trouble? Joseph had a dream, received it, and shared it, only to have trouble seeking him out because the enemy sought to hinder his destiny. However, God had a different plan in mind. It's important to understand that when God gives you a dream or promise, no demon, persecution, or anything can prevent it from being fulfilled except for you. That's why it's crucial not to let everyone speak into your eargates. Where there is a dream, there is a devil. And where there is a devil, there is the power of God within you to bind every demon in hell and send it back to where it belongs. Let the devil know that the place he once occupied is now null and void.

"Do you not know that your bodies are temples of the Holy Spirit, who is in you, whom you have received from God." - **1 Corinthians 3:16-17**

These are the moments when we must press in even more and seek God. You may say, "Well, I am seeking God, but my situation still appears unchanged, and I feel tired and drained." My brother or sister, one of the lessons life has taught me is that when we become weary and drained, it is often because we are trying to fight our battles in our own strength. The word of God reminds us to trust in the Lord with all our hearts, not relying on our own understanding but acknowledging Him in all our ways, and He will guide our paths. So, let us give all the glory to God, who has the power to keep us from stumbling and will bring us with great joy into His glorious presence without a single fault. All glory belongs to Him, the one and only God, our Savior Jesus Christ.

Unmerited Favor

*L*et us embark on a closer examination of favor. Favor not only rests upon you, but it also follows you wherever you go. It is akin to the symbolic coat of many colors that Jacob, Joseph's father, bestowed upon him. However, on a spiritual level, our Heavenly Father's divine power has graciously provided everything we need for life and godliness through the knowledge of Him, who called us to His own glory and excellence. Through His precious and magnificent promises, we can partake in the divine nature and escape the corruption that exists in the world due to sinful desires.

Listen closely; the moment you received Christ, the favor of God was bestowed upon you. And the approval, support, and liking of God are all you need to move forward with your dreams. When God placed His hand upon your life, He adorned you with a coat of many colors. This garment you wear is uncompromisable. The Father holds you accountable for every decision and action you take. It is of utmost importance that you fulfill the purposes of God in your life. As the Body of Christ—a body of believers—we don't have time to compromise, imitate, seek approval from others, or delay our destiny. There is a promise and a dream awaiting your pursuit.

When the Father extended His mercy to us, saving our souls from the corruption of sin, He clothed us in the coat of many colors—favor, righteousness, mercy, grace, holiness, love, kindness, forgiveness, and more. This coat represents extraordinary acts of kindness and favor. As I began to align myself with the ways and mindset of Christ, I witnessed supernatural power in action. It is favor that opened doors when people said no. It is favor that paid the light bill when the electricity should have been off. It was the favor of God that preserved our sanity when we should have lost our minds. It was the favor of God that shielded us from seen and unseen dangers—it was favor!

So, as you continue to rest upon God's promises and find inspiration in the words of exhortation throughout this book, I want you to be encouraged by the example of Joseph. When God looks upon you, He sees a heart that delights in Him; He sees a heart that longs to be by His side to know Him and seek understanding. The Father knows and sees you. You no longer need to question because the hand of the Lord has released favor upon your life, and it is no ordinary favor. It is the kind of favor that leaves you in awe, making you wonder and say, "This has never happened before!" Therefore, stay the course. Hold your ground. The Father seeks true worshipers who will worship Him in spirit and truth. Trust the process and continue to walk in the favor that God has graciously bestowed upon you.

Life and Godliness

What is life and godliness? To have life means I have been crucified with Christ, and I no longer live, but Christ lives in me. The life I now live in the body, I live by faith in the Son of God, who loved me and gave himself for me. This verse speaks of the suffering and endurance that follow a life of favor. There is no way one can expect to be covered in favor and not expect to face challenges. However, what you should be mindful of is that as God was with Joseph, so He is with you.

Understanding favor gives you an advantage, a divine empowerment, and a key to open up the right doors. Oftentimes, we use the word favor so carelessly that it sounds cliché. There are times when some have obtained favorable outcomes, thinking it was all on their own.

The downfall in it all is that when we get so comfortable with God and the blessings He bestows upon us, we lose the reverence and gratitude one is to have. I'm reminded of the moments I stand in my shower, telling God, thank you for the water He has allowed me to have, the soap I use to clean with, the toothpaste I'm able to brush my teeth, the eyes to see my children and grandchildren have, and the list goes on. One of the reasons my heart is often filled with gratitude is because of the mercy, grace, and favor of God. I've come to this realization that God didn't have to do anything, but He did. And every moment I get a chance, I just want to tell Him, "Thank you."

So, as you go throughout the day, be mindful of your coat. Guard and protect the garments you wear; they are very costly and valuable. Every color displayed in your garments makes mention of your name. The Father had your coat specially made for you, and each person's coat varies according to their purpose. Yet, it's still one and the same, exemplifying the favor and purposes of God. So, although the color of my coat displays a different design or pattern, we must not forget one thing: the experiences formed the pattern, but the result of the blessing is the same—the favor of God.

Let's take a brief look at the rainbow and how the radiance of its colors fills the land each time the promised rainbow appears. It's kind of like that with you and me. Whenever you show up in the fullness of who God appointed you to be, there is a radiance that follows you. And the favor that rests upon your life, none can deny because the glory of God will be upon you. When Joseph encountered opposition, the favor upon his life revealed the hand of the Lord each time.

And no matter how much the enemy plotted his demise, death, and defeat, they could not prevail. My brother or sister, you are equipped for the opposition. Every obstacle that is in your way, you have the power to speak to that mountain and command it to go. What are you going to do, Joseph? Are you going to hide and cry? Or are you going to take your weapons and fight? In the name of the Lord Jesus, I command you to get up and fight! Take dominion and fight! Get up! Get up! This is a war cry! I command you to get up and fight!

I understand your passion and desire to encourage and empower others to rise up and overcome their challenges. It's important to remember that, as believers, we have been equipped with spiritual weapons to stand against the schemes of the enemy. We have the power to speak to the mountains in our lives, trusting in the authority and victory we have through Christ.

However, it's also essential to approach these battles with wisdom, discernment, and reliance on God's guidance. We should seek His will and follow His leading in every situation. Fighting doesn't always mean physical confrontation or engaging in a visible battle. It can also involve standing firm in our faith, resisting temptation, and persevering through trials with the help of the Holy Spirit.

So, while I understand the call to rise up and fight, let's remember to do so in alignment with God's purposes, seeking His guidance and relying on His strength. We can trust that in His power and through His grace, we will overcome the challenges we face.

"And from the days of John the Baptist until now, the Kingdom of Heaven suffereth violence, and the violent take it by force."
-Matthew 11:12

"The kingdom of Heaven suffers violence" is a figurative expression referring to the multitude of people eagerly awaiting to hear God's word and witness the coming of the Messiah.

Therefore, it is crucial for you to persevere and not give up amidst opposition. Every obstacle that opposes you will be overcome when you rise up and embrace your calling, allowing the hand of the Lord to guide you in fulfilling your purpose and destiny. Your vibrant garments should reflect the fullness of who God created you to be. I admonish you to walk in your purpose and fulfill your divine destiny, as the favor of God has already gone before you.

Rashonda Henley

Rashonda Henley is a Charlotte-based entrepreneur, motivational speaker, and mentor for her audience. She began her career into medical science as a direct support professional and nurse's aide. After achieving a handful of corporate and on-the-field expertise in the healthcare field, she founded her own brand that provides health, food and nutrition services to her customers.

She started to pursue her degree at Davenport University. Since then, she started elevating her life. Her career right now is the accumulation of some core personal experiences of struggle, hard work, skills in communication, and problem-solving to empower others through motivational speaking, writing, and mentoring. But more than that, she is a dedicated mother of three and a grandmother of two, which gave her the confidence to understand the importance of being able to balance work and family life successfully. Her passion lies in empowering others to reach their full potential, which is why she also offers mentorship programs for young women who are seeking guidance on how to achieve their dreams. With that, her spectacular journey also incorporates Rashonda becoming a featured columnist in KISH magazine and has been interviewed by various media outlets such as Davenport University. When she is not found writing creative pieces of works, she enjoys spending time with her family and friends, reading the Bible, and volunteering at church. Other than that, her desire is to see people connect with God, elevate their lives, and touch the world around them. She is the ultimate epitome of a woman who knows her purpose and is living it out to the fullest. Hence, if you ever have the chance to meet her, you will instantly see her passion for life and love for people. She is truly a light in this world and is making a difference one person at a time.

Contact Information:

Email: rhenley328@yahoo.com
Facebook: Rashonda Henley.
7901 Lakehouse Lane Apt 1 Charlotte Nc 28210.

Keep Moving Forward

Ambassador Cenena Lowe

*L*ife has a way of presenting conflict and obstacles at unexpected times, doesn't it? As I'm reminded of the first major setback I encountered shortly after graduating high school, a pregnancy that forever altered the course of my life. Now, although my birth mom didn't raise me and because of that, I made a vow to keep and raise the twins. Yes, my first pregnancy was twins–double for your trouble. This is one of the setbacks that shaped my life forever in my opinion. You may have encountered several setbacks in life that were a transformative experience for you but even in the face of adversary, I learned one thing: the power to rise above lies within me. I am telling my story and hope that my story will remind you that the power you have to rise above lies within you.

I would like to ask you a question right now. Are there moments when you held on to the pain? In the process, did you regret holding on to that? Yes, my journey began with what you can say was an unexpected detour months after graduating high school. A pregnancy kind of turned my world upside down. I had plans to attend DeVry, a college in the fall, in Atlanta, GA. Months after graduating October 1994, myself and my cousin who her boyfriend later murdered had plans to move hours away and attend college. So, for me, having someone like a sister murdered at a young age at that time was also a setback that affected me in several ways. And I think now that the weekend she's murdered was the same weekend

I conceived. Wow. So, I had to shed the weight of my past and embrace the possibilities that lay ahead. Now that was not easy.

I made a choice to emerge by using, first of all, my voice. Just start choosing to move forward and not lay down in the situation and just die in the place that you are. Life is not based or measured by the number of times we fall but by how many times we rise again. Get Up! So, I could tell you so many examples as I'm ministering. Hello! If you have fallen, not at peace or in a dark place, I want to encourage you to get up. Every set-up served as a stepping stone. Life itself has a unique way of shaping us into the person that we are destined to become. To that single mother who finds herself in different relationships for many reasons and that single mother who finds herself in abusive relationships or an abusive marriage, I pray you find the courage to break free from the shackles of the abuse. "Don't let the shackles silence you." Sometimes, in abusive relationships and marriages, we as women or the one who's being abused, lose our voice. You are not alone, my beautiful sister, and you don't have to stay there. I was once a single mother, married to an abusive husband.

Can I encourage you? You are so much stronger than you think, and you have the power to walk away from and to overcome every challenge. Embrace the power that's within. First of all, believe in yourself. Believe that there is someone else out there that will love you and treat you the way that you should be treated. Believe in yourself. For you, my sister, possess greatness that knows no limits. You are beautiful. You are powerful. And most of all, you matter with or without a man. Sometimes, there is a journey to wholeness. It's not without any challenges, but it's a testament to your strength. So the timing is that we are not whole because there's a void that we are trying to fill. With every void I thought to fill was not an absence of external things, but an inner thing. Have you heard in the bible story of the woman with the issue of blood? She had inner bleeding. She was bleeding from the inside, and most of us are dealing with things on the inside. It's nothing to do with external, but it's inner, and through my struggles, I found myself making decisions rooted in the unworthiness and cycles of self-destruction that are definitely driven by a deep void within.

I believe any type of abuse can bring about a list of things. For one, low self-esteem can be brought about through being abused. So, have you ever noticed in a relationship or marriage or thought to yourself how much confidence and self-esteem you had before you got into this relationship? See, you are a strong and powerful person. If you had no problem missing your pinion and different things and suddenly you come into abusive relationships, it can do something to your self-esteem. Ever noticed that about yourself? I was so full of confidence before I got into this relationship. I believed in myself before I got into this marriage. Feeling unworthy is a burden that can weigh so heavily on your spirit. It can cloud your judgement and your vision. It can also cloud your thoughts. So, did you make an irrational decision? One thing I've learned is that relationships can build you up or tear you down.

For a minute, I found myself in many relationships that devalued me. So, I want to encourage someone reading this story right now. Someone else may not value you, but it does not mean you're not valuable. Some things we experience bring us into the realization that we are really stronger than what we think. One thing I want to say is that it's OK to struggle, and it's OK to feel lost. Sometimes, it's OK to feel like you want to give up on yourself. Sometimes, it's OK to feel misunderstood. Sometimes, it's just OK to feel this way. But one thing you don't need to do is give up on yourself. Bring yourself back into reality and know that you are worthy. You are very loved and worthy. You're worthy of peace. You're worthy of happiness. You're worthy of respect. In life, I've had many ups and downs, but all I can think of is that the favor of God was on my life the whole time. So, if you're reading this and struggling in any capacity, I want you to know that you are not alone. You have the power to overcome these challenges, although life will throw at you many things. But you can overcome; just believe in yourself. So, sometimes, we make decisions that make us feel broken or worthless.

Except for the struggle, we are often feeling alone and searching for something just to fill the void inside of us. But I really didn't know what it was when I was searching. I know now what it was. Now, I know it was because of rejection. I'm passionate about sharing my story with you, hoping it may inspire you and encourage you on your own journey. As life throws at you different challenges. One thing we know, there will always be pain and hardship until we go home to glory. But one thing I've learned is I will not and I refuse to let my past stop me from moving forward. Let me encourage you to do the same. Despite the past mistakes and all odds against me, a little girl from Mississippi, I managed to push through the hard, confused, painful, broken, and wounded times. This journey has not been easy, but it has taught me the importance of my coat. As I mentioned coat, I remember having a dream and in the dream that somebody actually tried to steal my coat. And in that, the spirit of the Lord said there is jealousy around you. So even when you don't feel as if you are favored, you are important or matter, the fact remains that they're jealous. There is jealousy around you, even when you don't think it because you think, who is jealous of me? Why would they be jealous of me?

But even if you don't feel you are favored or important, you have purpose, and the coat serves a purpose. Can I say this? Others see the spark, and some see the shine that you are wearing before you do. Your path may make you experience false accusations or people trying to kill your character and life. In order to get to the place of authority, you have to go through conflict. No one likes to go through or experience conflict, but trials and tribulations are a part of life. Oh, you have a coat of many colors. The coat belongs to you; no one can take it because it won't fit them. What God has designed for you is tailor-made, especially for you and you only. People will set out to destroy your life. You carry within you authority. Even in self-doubt, I still found my voice and my value. So let me encourage you. You may have a little doubt in yourself, but I pray as you read my story that you find your voice and your value. I know it seems like the more you push, the harder it gets, and the more you push, the more you are knocked down. There's an enemy that will try to strip you of everything that belongs to you. But Let me encourage you; the enemy cannot keep you down. Everyone is about to see the coat and what the father has for you. Life will throw at you conflict, but keep moving forward.

Ambassador Cenena Lowe

Cenena Lowe is an anointed, appointed, dynamic deliverer of the word of God. She has been called by God to teach and preach the life-changing Word of Jesus Christ. She is a true Kingdom Intercessor and Worshiper who is a powerful yet graceful force in the kingdom of God. She is known to be an influential leader who serves with excellence, integrity and has a loving, caring demeanor, and passion for people with intense love of family.

With a unique heart and anointing for women, Ambassador Lowe is the founder of Women Of Youth Outreach Ministries, Inc. She specializes in empowering Women from all walks of life, and she has dedicated much of her ministry to leading women to wholeness through prayer, personal development, and spiritual direction.

Ambassador Cenena's goal is to build up the body of Christ through the ministry of teaching and preaching (**Ephesians 4:11**) and to share the love of God to a hurting world. Cenena has been a guest speaker on the Fierce, Ignition and Activation Show with Dr. Deborah Allen on Envisioned Broadcasting Radio and also a guest speaker on Fierce TV on DominionTV, as a special guest with Dr. Deborah Allen.

Cenena has been a guest on the Stella award-winning radio station, "The Morning Show with the Bishop." Cenena has also been featured in K.I.S.H. magazine as the Top 22 Influential Trailblazers 2022 edition. Cenena is a 2 times International best-seller author. Ambassador Cenena is an inspirational speaker called to empower people. She is also the proud mother of two sons and one daughter.

Faith: What was Designed to Kill Me Built Me

Dr. Tameka Stanford-Daniels

Hebrews 11:1, "Now faith is the substance of things hoped for, the evidence of things not seen." (KJV)

Walking by faith is hard for many to do; we want to know the direction, we want to know most of the details, and we want to see with our eyes what's going to happen while walking by faith. Trusting God in the midst of the faith walk can be challenging, especially when everything else around you seems the opposite. Well, here's a few highlights of my stories: how my faith was birthed, how I had no choice but to walk by faith. I had no choice but to trust God along the way… It seemed as if the odds were against me and that God placed me in a situation where even my family couldn't and wouldn't help me. God allowed my faith to become activated through my circumstances, through my challenges, and through the many hard trials in my life.

Although I didn't always understand what God was doing through me, I believed in God, his word and everything God spoke concerning me, which increased my faith. This is what made me realize that what was Designed to kill me Built me.

From being homeless with 3 children, living in shelters, to suffering with a severe case of eczema, to going through in relationships and so much more. There were times I cried, I screamed, and at one point, I felt invisible. Yes, you heard me INVISIBLE! Like can people see me? The pain, the suffering, the humiliation, the shame, the ridicule, the rejection, the loneliness, all of this built my faith. It was by faith that God brought me through. It was by faith that God healed my body. It was by faith that God brought me from homeless to homeowner. It was by faith that God allowed me to be found and happily married for 14 years faithfully to my husband. It was by faith God took away my shame and brought me to a place of honor. It was by faith that God took me from welfare to owning several successful businesses. It is by faith that God took me from what the world considers nobody to God's Apostle, Prophet, Teacher, Pastor and Evangelist. It was by faith through my Lord and Savior Jesus Christ that God forgave me, saved and cleansed me.

I am blessed to be a living testimony to you that is reading this; that by FAITH, God in all his RIGHTEOUSNESS is ABLE to do ALL THINGS except FAIL. Even when you think your life is so jacked-up and unfixable, I come to tell you that your life is repairable, and what you consider unrepairable is an opportunity for God to get the Glory out of your life, using everything you have been through to make you a living testimony just like he has done for me.

I, Dr. Tameka Stanford-Daniels, come to tell you that GOD is ABLE if you BELIEVE.

It wasn't just my change of lifestyle; it was my faith in God through my relationship with Jesus. Even when I did not understand, I continued to seek God daily, read the Word, spend time with God, and pray and fast. Being consistent in all of this built me in the midst of what I was going through, so even when the enemy had plans to steal, kill and destroy me, it did not work! My faith along with my time spent with the Father, being consistent with reading, praying and fasting, the enemy's plan could not prosper against me. He wanted me to die, but God saw to it that I live. The devil wanted you to die, but God saw to it that you LIVED.

What was Designed to Kill you will Build You.

Acknowledgements

I would like to acknowledge my Heavenly Father, who is the head of my life and has made this opportunity possible.

I would like to acknowledge my husband, Al for being the GREATEST cheerleader, always seeing the best in me no matter what, THANK YOU!

To my Blessed children Shar'Ron, Veronica, Jecavis, THANK YOU for your continued love and support.

To Pastor Shannell Coverdale, my niece, THANK YOU for all you have done to assist me!!

To my Mother, Cheryl Bryant, Thank you for being that greatest example in my life. My STRENGTH comes from what you have always DEMONSTRATED. MOMMY, THANK YOU for EVERYTHING!!!

Apostle Dr. Tameka Stanford-Daniels

Apostle Dr. Tameka Stanford-Daniels, is an emerging Apostolic Leader on the Rise, Certified Christian Counselor, motivational speaker, teacher, and prophetic minister known as the Transformation Specialist.

She is the founder of Sarai's Daughters International Ministry, Crusade Deliverance Ministry of Faith, and Flaming Swords of Fire Global Ministries located in New Castle and Dover, Delaware.

Ministry isn't all of who she is! It's just a facet of how she's impacting the earth.

A businesswoman indeed with a passion for people! She has built and established several businesses from her Daycare Center, "MUM MUM Meka's" to her financial and life consultation services. In her most recent works, a community center, "Stanford Community Development Corporation", a Substance Use & Mental Health Clinic that will service the greater Dover, De and surrounding areas.

Contact Dr. Tameka Stanford-Daniels

dr.tamekastanforddaniels@gmail.com
Facebook: DrTameka Daniels
Instagram: DrTameka Daniels
302-241-6953

A God Given Dream will take you Deeper!!!

Prophetess Shirlene Jones

*B*e prepared to walk in total obedience. Start by covering yourself with the BLOOD of JESUS, pray as you think, then begin to write and speak scripture aloud in your hearing. It is with great pleasure that I accept my assignment to encourage you to Go Deeper in your GOD-Given Dreams (what you are anointed and destined by GOD to do)! Get excited, write, and go forth as the SPIRIT gives you the flow.

As I read about Joseph's life, it started with him as a young man of seventeen, and he was a Dreamer!!! We find Joseph tending the flock (sheep) with his brothers; catch this: Joseph was already being groomed/prepared by GOD for Purpose. Joseph was loved/favored by his father (Israel) more than his brothers; his brothers hated him for that and could speak kindly to him. Initially, it seemed as if Joseph would be the least likely to succeed, possibly because he had revealed his GOD-Given Dreams way too soon. However, Joseph trusted GOD much more than he knew, more than what he could see, and even more than the contempt that his own family felt regarding him. As we press towards the mark of the prize (eternal life in Christ JESUS) of the higher calling, it is imperative that we Trust GOD far beyond what we can see.

As Joseph revealed his GOD-Given Dreams to his family, he expressed several things that he had seen; but in every dream, Joseph rose and became

63

greater than his family. In one instant, Joseph's father rebuked him. He was the younger brother of the family and eventually, he would be promoted to rule over all his brothers and his father too. Increasingly, his brother showed more blatant hatred towards him. Just like GOD did in Joseph's life, HE is going to increase your sphere of influence because the plan that HE has created for you is greaterthan you could ask or even imagine.

Yes, it did appear as though Joseph had revealed his dream way too soon, but being rejected by his family was all a part of Joseph's Pruning Process (GOD'S plan to bring Joseph to an expected end!). The Process is a primary component of GOD'S timing, which is Always Perfect.

One characteristic that we will discover is that Joseph never compared himself to his brothers nor anyone else. Joseph was not arrogant nor inflated with pride; he simply shared his GOD Given-Dreams. Think about this: when we compare ourselves to others, it is self-sabotage. Allow GOD to shape your thoughts; you have to cast down negative imaginations and any thought that is puffed up in nature. Comparison causes self-doubt; as we journey, we will learn to trust GOD'S plan for our lives more than our own.

You may think or even say, but GOD, "I am not qualified; I don't know how to do this or that."

Everyone in the Bible could have given GOD an excuse as to why they did meet the qualifications to be used by HIM. Considering all that Joseph faced in the beginning, he could have started complaining and doubt would have been his portion. Joseph could have given up or given in, or completely given out (fainted) under the pressure of being rejected by his family. Remember, Joseph was seventeen years old. To be rejected means to refuse to accept, consider, receive, or hear. (Webster's dictionary) We must recognize that being rejected is a part of life's process. At times, we will be abandoned, cast aside, or even discarded. But that's the reason why we do not entertain any negative thoughts. **2 Corinthians 10:5 KJV**, "Casting down imaginations, and every high thing that exalteth itself against the knowledge of GOD, an bringing into captivity every thought to the obedience of Christ."

If we lack wisdom and confidence, the Bible states that we can ask. **James 1:5-6 NIV**, "If any of you lacks wisdom, you should ask GOD, who givens generously to all without finding fault, and it will given to you. But when you ask, you must believe and not doubt, because one who doubts is like a wave in the sea, blown and tossed by the wind."

An aspect of seeing your GOD-Given Dreams come to fruition is to wait on HIM. Do not sit murmuring and complaining, but remain diligent and faithful to your current Kingdom assignment. Go forth and know that a good man's steps are ordered by the LORD.

Joseph was thrown into a pit by his brothers; they told their father that Joseph had succumbed to an attack by an animal. You may or may not be thrown into a physical pit, but just know that the devil will have your opposers set a trap for you, too. At times, life may appear to be tossing one hurdle for you to overcome after the another….. **Romans 8:31 NIV**, "What, then, shall we say in response to these things? If GOD is for us, who can be against us?"

Joseph was taken out of the pit, only to be sold into slavery by these same brothers. Please take notice of Joseph's disposition as one wretched event after another continued to unfold in his life. But there is an extraordinary pattern to Joseph's behavior; his Trust in GOD was unwavering. The pit that satan (enemy) has devised for you may be a physical disease (some type of sickness: cancer, kidney disease, diabetes, HIV, or Aids) or mental illness (for instance: bipolar, depression, anxiety, or even schizophrenia}, or fornication, adultery, stealing, lying, or holding strife, bitterness, and anger in your heart. These are just some examples of the many pitfalls that satan desires to entrap us in.

GOD elevated and prospered Joseph in the house of Potiphar (one of Pharaoh's officials). Potiphar could see that GOD was with Joseph. I promise you that just like Joseph, people will see the Hand of GOD on your life; some people will bless you; some will hate you, and not fully understand why.

Potiphar's wife was very attracted to Joseph, she desired him, but Joseph loved GOD so much that he would not sin against HIM. Joseph would not compromise his relationship with ABBA FATHER. **Psalm 119:10,11 NIV**, "I seek YOU with my heart; do not let me stray from YOUR commands. I have hidden YOUR word in my heart that I might not sin against YOU."

So, Potiphar's wife lied against Joseph because he wouldn't lie down with her. Instead of having Joseph killed, Potiphar had him imprisoned. Everywhere Joseph I went, the favor of GOD rested on his life, even behind the prison walls. Jospeh was given charge (authority) over the other prisoners, as he was the servant to the captain of the guards. Because of his relationship with GOD, Joseph was able to minister to the other prisoners and the guards. How many of us can say if GOD allowed you to be falsely detained that you would be able to encourage others while serving a prison sentence? **Isaiah 26:3 NIV**, "You will keep in perfect peace those whose minds are steadfast because they trust in YOU."

For years and years, Joseph was displaced in one unstable setting after another, but wait for it!! GOD is going to cause a sudden shift in the trajectory of Joseph's life. Listen, Joseph never moved ahead of GOD, but he remained faithful as GOD processed him. The Process is necessary, and it may consist of being crushed and pruned until it is no longer our will, but we allow GOD to be LORD over our life. Does it not feel good? No, but it will work together for your good. When GOD speaks over your life, it shall surely come to pass because HIS Plan is Always Better!!! Trust HIM!! **Psalm 34:8 NIV**, "Taste and see that the LORD is good; blessed is the one who takes refuge in HIM."

Amidst the haters and his afflictions, Joseph continued to walk in total obedience to the task set before him. Joseph's afflictions brought him to a great place of anointing and prominence.

Afflictions activate heaven; GOD allows it because afflictions promote growth.

Joseph's GOD-Given Gift of interpreting dreams manifested while he was in prison, and it sealed his future. The manifestation of his prophetic giftings enabled Joseph to minister to two of Pharaoh's household servants, the chief Baker and the chief Butler, who were imprisoned with him. Joseph interpreted both of their dreams; the Chief Baker was beheaded three days later, while the Chief Butler was returned to his post. Joseph asked them to remember him when they were restored to Pharaoh's house. A few years past, Joseph had been forgotten. But there arose an occasion when Pharaoh had a dream, and no one (not a magician nor the wise men) could interpret it. Finally, the Chief Butler remembered Joseph. Joseph was brought to Pharaoh's house and he was groomed before being presented to Pharaoh.

When Joseph stood before Pharaoh, he asked Joseph if he could interpret his dream? Joseph said, "no, I cannot, but GOD can give you the answer to your dream." GOD revealed that the dreams were the same: there would be seven years of plenty followed by seven years of famine. So, Pharaoh promoted Joseph and placed his signet ring on Joseph's finger; he dressed him in robes of fine linen and put a gold chain around his neck. Joseph rode in a chariot and was second-in-command. Joseph was even given a new name Joseph was thirty years old, and GOD gave him the strategy of how to grow and store the provisions for the famine. Joseph did marry an Egyptian woman, and he had two sons.

People from all over the world had to come to Egypt to purchase food to survive, even Joseph's family and he recognized them. But, instead of cursing or taking advantage of them, he forgave them and united with them. Throughout his life, Joseph looked to the Author and the Finisher of his faith. Hallelujah!! I say to you, "Lift up your heads, O ye gates; And be ye lifted up, ye everlasting doors; And the KING of GLORY shall come in. Who is this KING of GLORY? The LORD strong and mighty, the LORD mighty in battle." **Psalm 24:7-8**

Joseph was satisfied in GOD, meaning he was set apart for GOD. GOD is a Consuming FIRE and We need to allow HIM to burn the residue of the world off. We are in the world but not of the World. GOD will always permit us to make our own choices to align with HIS will or our own.

Joseph was a splendid example of one who followed GOD' plan, purpose, and will to reach his destiny. As we press towards the promises of GOD and believe in the manifestation of our dreams, let's trust the Process. Please do not get caught up in the plan, plot, scheme, or tricks satan has devised against you; no pity parties, murmuring, or complaining. In this season, we must emerge from the pit, the prison, and return to the palace.

Speak life over yourself every day!!!

This is the hour for us to walk in Divine Purpose; stop making GOD small; HE is the GREAT I AM, HE is HIGH AND LIFTED UP; HE is the LIFTER of our head; HE is FAITHFUL; He is the ALPHA and the OMEGA, HE is the AMAZING GRACE!!!

$\mathit{Shirlene\ Jones\ Acknowledgements}$

First and foremost, I want to give all Glory and Honor to my LORD and SAVIOR, JESUS; without HIM, this would not have been possible!! I quote this scripture often because it brings me back to ground zero (not in my own strength: **Proverbs 3:5-6,** "Trust in the LORD with all of thine heart and lean not to thine own understanding. (6) In all thy ways acknowledge him, and he shall direct thy paths."

In loving memory of my beautiful mother, Shirley Elizabeth Jones. I am so grateful to have had a strong loving Mom who prayed, encouraged, and supported me.

In memory of my father, Frank Reginald Olivis Jr., I am thankful for his encouragement, love, and the wisdom that he always imparted.

To my handsome son and beautiful daughter, Jerome Jr., and Jasmine, I love you both sincerely. Thank you, guys, so much for always keeping me on my A-game!!!

To my five handsome grandsons, KajMere, Jerome III, Jeremy, Jerron, Caelan, and a new great-granddaughter, Simira, I love all of you dearly!!!

To my handsome stepson, Branden Hayman Jackson: I love you, and thank you so much for sending me special gifts.

To Cyndi and Andrea, you guys are the bomb when it comes to sisters; I am so super grateful that GOD gave me the two of you!!! To Timmy, my baby brother, you will always be that dude; to Randy, truly we thank GOD for the yes in your spirit!! Charlotte, Anna, and Reg (Frank III), Granny Joyce: I love all of you; thank you so much for our wonderful talks and your prayers!!!

A special thank you, Teresa Winstead-Finney and Delores Anderson, for your love, prayers, and always being in my corner!!

Thank you so much Dr. Kishma George for the encouragement and the push to go deeper!!!

Prophetess Shirlene Jones

Shirlene Jones is a native Delawarean. She has both an adult son and daughter, as well as five grandsons.

In 2008, GOD used Shirlene to birth out S.O. S.A.D. Outreach Ministry (Save Our Sons And Daughters), a street ministry. The foundational scripture are **Matthews 6:33** and **Luke 10:2**. The aim of this ministry is to assist in any capacity to stop the violence among Delaware's youth and young adults. Shirlene under the umbrella of S.O. S.A.D., has hosted numerous Back to School Celebrations for At-Risk youth and their families to celebrate Learning, Life, and Love! Over the decade, S.O. S.A.D. Outreach Ministry has provided more than 700 Backpacks w/supplies according to grade level and over 4000 lbs. of food to needy families in and around Kent County, DE.

Shirlene is an Intercessor; she prayed and shared the Word of GOD on a Prophetic Empowerment Prayer Call on a weekly basis for several years. She hosted an Annual Women's Conference titled "ARISE." Shirlene currently hosts "The WORD Empowers" every Tuesday morning at 7:00 AM EST. on Facebook Live.

Shirlene has an Associate degree in Criminal Justice and a Bachelor's degree in Sociology; she is a Certified Drug and Alcohol Counsel both in Delaware and nationally, and also she is a Licensed Social Worker. She has a varied background in the Human Services field, having worked as a Substance Abuse Counselor in the Dept. of Corrections, a Wraparound Therapist in Mental Health, and a Substance Educator in a Delaware Detention Center. She currently working for Amerihealth Caritas of Delaware as a Resource Coordinator. Shirlene has volunteered at a Code Purple Women's Shelter since 2017.

Shirlene has been featured in the Delaware State News, KISH Magazine, New Being Queen Magazine, Dominion TV - "The DREAMER in You", Elevation TV - "FIERCE."

Co-Author of Birthing the DREAMER in You and Prophecy Stories, Vol. 1.

Shirlene is an active member of Calvary Church in Dover, a motivational speaker, mentor, author, and very passionate about winning souls for the Kingdom of GOD.

Shirlene proclaims, "when nothing else would help, it was JESUS' love that lifted me!!"

The Word is your Sword!

Claudine Noel

I shall live and not die! Those were the words that I could remember uttering as I lay in my hospital bed after experiencing a stroke at work. There were so many other words fluttering my mind as I tried to understand what had happened to me and will I ever walk again? If it wasn't for the word of God and the encouragement of others through their comforting words of "You will walk again," I don't think I would have recovered as I have after experiencing a blood vessel popping in my brain, which caused me to have the stroke and resulted to my left side befalling weak. **Luke 4:1-13**, tells us of the story of Christ being led by the Holy Spirit into the wilderness for 40 days and 40 nights. There, He was tempted by the devil for those 40 days. He had been without food for quite some time, and in the midst of his weak state, the enemy popped up and said to him, "If you are the Son of God turn these rocks into bread" **(Lk 4:3)**. Then Christ says "It is written, Man shall not live by bread alone. But by every *Word* of God" **(Matt 4:4)**. Then the devil tries to tempt Christ again by showing Christ the world and all that is in it **(Lk 4:5-6)**. Then in verse 7, he proceeds to tell Christ, "This can be yours if you worship me." Christ responds by saying in verse 8, "Get thee behind me Satan, *it is written*, you shall worship the Lord your God and Him only you shall serve. Then Satan comes and tries to challenge Christ with the word by bringing Christ into a high place and tells Christ to

73

throw himself down if He is the Son of God because *it is written* that He shall give His angels charge over you to keep you **(Ps 91:11-12)**. Christ answers with Deuteronomy 6:16: It has been said, "You shall not tempt the Lord your God."

There are three truths I would like to convey from this story. First truth, the word of God is very powerful in itself. We saw Christ in a very vulnerable state; He was weak, had not eaten for days, and we can imagine perhaps very tired as well. Now, here comes the devil trying to tempt him at a time of weakness and vulnerability; that's what the enemy does to us. He comes when we are at our weak point, at a time when we are vulnerable, and begins to tempt us and persuade us to do his will and not God's will, and his will brings us into a life of sin, depression, emptiness, living a life of poverty and brokenness. We find that Christ does not use large, elaborate words. He states what the word of His Father God says and punches the enemy with it. Every time Christ said *it is written,* that was an uppercut to Satan. The word of God has so much power that the author of Hebrews writes how the word of God is sharper than A two-edged sword, it is living and powerful **(Hebrew 4:12)**. When the enemy himself or uses people around you as his game piece to bring destruction within your life, remember that with the word of God You can slay him for the coward that he is.

The second truth that emerges out of this story is that Jesus spoke with authority and assurance. He knew the power of the living word. This is why it is important for us to read the word of God–our Bibles. It contains keys, aka scriptures to our freedom and deliverance from the plans of Satan. When he's trying to kill your dream of that business you want/need to start, when he's trying to kill and steal your destiny, when he's trying to harm your family, when he's trying to tear down that vision, that dream that you know God gave you in the midnight hour – Your WORD, God's Word are the keys, the Word of God is your **SWORD** to slay the enemy and all his plans against your life.

The third truth is Satan knew the power behind the statement of "*it is written.*" The word of God is the breath of God, the Spirit of God, and in the breath of God, there is life and life abundantly. Use the word of God as your sword to free you from the chains, the shackles, and the lies of the enemy in every sector of your life.

Be The Example

There are two times in my life that I can remember when I had to take a stand for what was right or to be an example. The first one was when I was in college; I volunteered for this nonprofit called Young Life. And every year, we would take kids to different campsites they had. Part of the camping experience was to do this obstacle course that would help and teach them to face their fears not only in the physical aspect but in the spiritual aspect. One of the campers was so scared. She was so nervous she was crying she did not want to get on the ropes course; as a matter of fact, I didn't either. She was crying on the outside. I was yelling and crying on the inside. But I knew I needed to be an example to her to take the leap and face my fears of heights and just go. I knew I needed to be the example to her, to let her know that it was safe and secure, that at the end of the day, God got you and we, the staff, got you; your safety is our concern. The other time was when I was working for this manufacturing company, and we just appointed a new VP of Manufacturing. In the first few weeks, it was a little hectic. I had to learn him as a boss; moreover, he had to learn me as an employee. There was a big order that fell through the cracks. I couldn't figure out where the breakdown of communication was. This was something that was costing the company thousands of dollars. After several attempts of trying to figure out where the mistake was, how and why it was made and coming to a dead end, I finally stepped into my VP's office and said it was my fault; I take full responsibility for this mishap. Not knowing what the outcome would be, I knew someone from our department had to take responsibility and put a solution in place so this mistake would not happen again.

This reminds me of the story of Esther in the Bible. She was tasked with a great responsibility to go before the king and to plead for her people, knowing that there was a strong possibility that she would perish in doing so. In Esther chapter four, we learn how Mordechai, her uncle, informs her of Haman's plot to destroy the Jewish people in the country. Upon learning of this tragedy, Esther gives her uncle instructions to have all the Jewish people in the land fast for three days and three nights with no food or water. As she herself fasted three days and three nights with no food or water along with her servants because she knew the great danger that she was about to embark on, going before the king without being summoned by the king to plead her case before King Ahasuerus and revealing that she too, being Jewish was a death sentence. Esther became an example of what bravery and stepping out on faith looks like. Too many times, we, as children of God, forget the promises of God. The Word of God is filled with instructions on how to achieve our goals, projects, dreams, and visions. We allow the voice of the enemy to cause us to sit and delay our time concerning the gifts and talents that God has planted within us to be manifested in the earth realm. In **Matthew 17:20-20**, it reminds us and instructs us to have faith like a mustard seed. In **John 14:13-17**, it teaches us that whatever we ask in His name shall be so. In **Zachariah 4:6**, we are taught that it is not by might nor power but by the Lord's Spirit–that we will be able to accomplish our projects, dreams, and visions. Via a little bit of faith as small as a mustard seed, being bold to go before God to ask him what you need and what you desire and to remember that it is not by your power, it is not by your will, it is not by what you can do, but it is by remembering that it is only through the power of the Holy Spirit that God can give you strategic instructions to get through the forest of distractions and let-downs that the enemy posts before you. Your gift is needed in the earth realm; there is somebody that's waiting to be delivered, to be set free by the product and ministry that God has laid within you. Just like Esther remembered the words that her uncle said to her, "*Yet who knows whether you have come to the kingdom for such a time as this time*" (**Esther 4:14***).* It is not by happenstance that you desire or feel this weight to put out that book, maybe even write a screenplay or to start that restaurant or that food truck. It is not a coincidence that God has laid in your heart to help the disabled to go and pray with those in Hospice. What is within you has been laid inside you by the hand, the very breath of God to be manifested in the earth realm for the good of His Kingdom. Remember, you have been equipped and that the word of God is your sword to tear down the enemy and everything else standing in your way as you walk, run, and march into your place of next.

The Miseducation of Ruth

Growing up, I always felt like I was misunderstood. When I was younger, I had a little bit of a stuttering problem and also a lisp. I always pronounced Burger King wrong. I was very expressive with my facial features; I wore my emotions on my sleeve. When I spoke passionately about something I cared about, I was told I was yelling. When I got to college, I always felt like I was the oddball in the midst of the sisterhood we had become since we met in the long lines of registration as Class of 2003 at Bennett College. I would always have to explain what I meant or reiterate what I had just said two minutes ago. I had to explain why I did certain things because of my culture being Haitian American. I walked differently because of my knocked knees. I was always the tallest girl in my class up until Jr. high school. I was plus size the majority of my life; I went all throughout my life feeling misunderstood, until one day I woke up and something inside me said you are enough! Just the way you are, the way you speak and walk. I realized God created me for His purpose and His purpose alone.

There's a book in the Old Testament that we all know. She is the hero or "Shero" to all those who are waiting on their husbands, their Boaz.

The book of Ruth became the backbone of several singles conferences across the Christian community. "Wait on your Boaz," they would say. "God will send your Boaz," another would say. "Your Boaz is coming," the preacher would say. But when I begin to read Ruth for a 3rd, 5th and 6th time, I discovered there were several more stories to Ruth than just being *the woman Who ended up marrying a rich man*. I was miseducated on the story of Ruth. The first time God gave me a revelation of what was hidden behind the story of Ruth, He showed me how the Holy Spirit was spearheading Ruth and creating her story without her even knowing. The second time around, God had revealed another hidden secret within the book of Ruth to me. We begin with **Ruth 1:16**, *"Where you go, I will go, where you lodge, I will lodge. Your people shall be my people and your God, My God."* These are the words that Ruth expressed to her mother-in-law when Naomi was leaving Moab to go back to Judah after her husband and two sons died. Ruth was a powerhouse in ways people would consider as weak; she was a widow, a daughter-in-law to Naomi, childless for a period of time, obedient, selfless, meek, brave, content, and destined for greatness. She never questioned her mother-in-law and did not worry what others might think of her. She showed unconditional love; she put herself to the side to express God's love for her mother-in-law and for the people of God by allowing the Holy Spirit to do what He needed to do in her life. Ruth was more blessed because of her obedience and sacrifice. Ruth not only married a rich man, but Ruth's DNA also got to be part of the bloodline of Christ. Do not miss the blessings of God because you feel or society says you are different. Remember, the Holy Spirit is The Gift that Christ left for us here on earth to guide us and reveal the mysteries of heaven to us so they can be manifested here in the earth realm. Do not let the enemy distract you and lie to you, making you think you are too old, too young, too tall, too short, too dark in skin color, too shy, too loud, or too anything to move in the direction that God Himself is leading. Move in the spirit of faith, boldness, and confidence of Esther, who was willing to risk her life for her people. Take a step in the direction of Ruth through her obedience to elders, giving her keys of wisdom; she succeeded in a relationship that placed her in the lines of royalty despite her background as a Moabite. People all over the world are waiting on your gift, your vision, to break them free and or bring them comfort.

Your Rock is your Gift

Sitting in a boardroom meeting one day, I began to look all around the room; there were VPs, COOs, Managers, and Supervisors. I thought to myself, how did I end up at this table? I graduated college with a degree in Mass Communications, never thinking that I was going to end up in manufacturing as a career. I started at that company at the entry-level as an assistant to the production coordinator. Only to find myself a couple of years later at a table listening, learning, and gleaning from individuals who are seasoned in their respective sectors of the company without having the credentials of an MBA. I realized I only had a seat at the table because of the gifts that God had laid within me. You, too, can have a seat at the table in the respective area that God has called you or is calling you into.

Let's look at a story we are familiar with: the story of David and Goliath. David, the youngest out of all his siblings, served as a sheep herder for his father. Later on, in **1 Samuel 17**, we read how David would travel back and forth to the army camp to bring his brothers, who were fighting for King Saul, food and supplies. There came a period of 40 days where a giant from the opposing country named the Philistines was challenging King Saul and his army. King Saul sent men out to go and fight the giant of the Philistines; however, no one could face this great Philistine giant until David volunteered. He didn't go into the fight with the AK 47; David didn't go with tankers or a cannon bomb; even the army uniform David couldn't carry into the valley where the fight was to take place. He went into the fight with a slingshot and a few smooth stones, and with one stone on his first attempt, David was able to hit Goliath straight in his forehead, and down Goliath the Giant went. God gave David a seat at the warrior's table through his obedience of instruction from his father Jesse **(1Sam 17:17-19)** and David remembering God delivered him in the small battles **(1Sam 17:37)** before he said surely, He shall deliver the giant who mocks his people into his hands.

David was fueled by the understanding that this battle was not his but God's battle. **(1 Sam 17:47)** Furthermore, David remembered the training that he had in the wilderness while tending to his father's sheep. When a lion and a bear would take a sheep, he would strike them with a stone and then later on be able to eliminate them if need be. Therefore, remembering his training and knowing that with God on his side, this fight between him and Goliath was as sure on his side as he was sure of God being the living God of Israel. Just like David had a slingshot and a smooth rock in his hand to slay Goliath, you as well have a rock and a slingshot to annihilate the Goliaths in your life. That rock and slingshot is the gift that God has laid inside of you. That gift of being able to cook, the gift of being able to sing, the gift of being able to write books, screenplays, putting magazines and journals together. Those are your rocks that God has given you to be able to slay the Goliaths in your life. The Goliath of poverty, the Goliath of living from paycheck to paycheck, the Goliath of generational curses, the Goliath of sickness and disease. What do you need? The rock that you need is already in your hands.

Your Ability Is Your Worship

Since I was a little girl, I had the biggest wish to be able to sing with a beautiful voice. As I got older, I not only wanted to sing where my voice was beautiful, but I wanted to sing like the angels. I wanted to sing with power to break the walls of the enemy in the spirit world where my voice would be a battering ram against the plans of the enemy. But I sit here today still with the little crackling voice; sometimes I hit a good note; I can hold the note absolutely without a doubt. However, I came to learn that it doesn't matter how angelic my voice sounds, how I can go up and down on a music scale, if I could do vibratos or not. It is a fact that my wanting to come and sing before the Lord for His goodness and His mercy is worship enough for His ears. Because through my singing, I'm building the relationship, I'm coming to him just as I am, the way he wants me to. Are you worshipping God the way He would like you to? Worship is more than reading your word, praying a 5-minute prayer, and going to church for an hour or two. Worship is coming into a place where it's you and God, and you're submitting your whole self to our Lord and Savior. From having conversations with him to singing a song about Him, to Him, for Him, and to doing the very feat He's called us to do.

In **Luke Chapter 7:37-38**, we find a woman in the city that they called a sinner. She knew that Jesus was going to sit at the table in the Pharisee's house. She brought her alabaster box/flask of fragrant oil and stood at His feet behind him weeping, and she began to wash his feet with her tears and wiped them with the hair on her head, and she kissed his feet. She anointed them with the fragrant oil. The fragrant oil was an indispensable commodity in the ancient near East for food, medicine, fuel, and rituals. Oil was considered a blessing given by God. Thus, that oil was precious to that woman known as a sinner. But she saw fit to come and use the whole flask on the feet of Christ that was probably dirty from walking all day.

Nonetheless, that is all she had in her hands to bless the one that she knew had come to save her. She used what was in her hands. She used her source of income to put food on the table, her bartering tool for essential items. But she took what was precious to her and offered it up to the Lord, which became her worship. Please understand that within you as the creation of God, that there are several tools that God has buried within you to equip you for the achievements that He needs, even wants and desires in this earth realm. That gift, that talent that you have, the gift of being able to pack luggage neatly, the gift of being able to teach those that have learning disabilities; that is your worship unto God; to walk in the very deeds that He's called you to do, in the marketplace, on your job or at your place of worship. That is your most honorable, distinctive way to give God the glory and the honor. By doing the very deeds that He's called you to. Don't sit on your gift for another month. Don't sit on your gift for another decade, listening to the enemy's lies, being distracted by the pitfalls he's put in your life. Don't let the day come, when you stand before God and allow Him to show you the gifts and the gems that he had placed within you are still inside of you–gifts He was waiting for you to birth in the earth through you. Let your main goal be to leave this earth empty when you return back to our Lord and Savior, Jesus Christ. Heaven is waiting for you to move into your destiny. Heaven is excited to see you flow in that ocean of talent. Remember, there are people in the earth realm waiting for you to be delivered and set free through the gifts and talents sitting in your hands.

Claudine Noel

Claudine Noel is a Haitian-American native of Spring Valley, NY. She is the daughter of Mr. Jean-Claude and Nicole Noel, a big sister to David and Alexander Noel, and an auntie to several nieces and nephews.

In 2003, Claudine graduated from Bennett College for Women in Greensboro, NC, with a Bachelor of Arts degree in Mass Communications. Upon graduation, she worked with Young Life Greensboro outreach ministries from May 2003 to May 2006. She began a career in manufacturing in January 2008.

Claudine was licensed as a Minister of the Gospel by Shiloh Baptist Church in Plainfield, NJ. She served as one of the ministers in The *New Young Peoples Department* (N.Y.P.D) ministry. Claudine believes one should develop a solid foundation of one's relationship with Christ at a very young age in order to have a sound and strong Christian life in the future; her life shall be and is dedicated to this task. Today, she is under the mentorship of Apostle Jeffrey & Pastor Shanell Thompson of Deliverance to Kingdom Building Ministries in Somerset, NJ.

In addition, Claudine is a mentor to young adult women in various states; she is a conference speaker, an entrepreneur, and a private investor.

Contact Information

CLAUDINE NOEL

EMAILS: chosenvesselworship2021@gmail.com or thenoelgroupllc@gmail.com

WEBSITE: thenoelgroupllc.inteletravel.com

YOUTUBE CHANNEL: C's CORNER

INSTAGRAM: CCCs.CORNER

Purpose and Destiny Is My Name

Dr. Gail James

I knew I was born with purpose when the pain I experienced almost killed me. It's almost like trauma, pain, rejection, abandonment, and turmoil were my portion. I felt like I was the red-headed stepchild in the family. But I am still standing today because of my faith in God. I cannot give anyone else the glory. The faithfulness, grace and mercy of God are what kept me.

I have always felt like I was different from everyone else. It was like I was picked out to be picked on. My childhood was so traumatizing that I felt it was better if I would just die. The sexual abuse and molestation by three of my brothers, the domestic violence of three relationships and the physical abuse and rejection from my mother were traumatizing enough to cause me to attempt to kill myself. I felt there was no reason to live, so I attempted suicide by taking a bottle of Tylenol, which did nothing but make me vomit. When the Tylenol didn't work, I tried drinking bleach and that didn't kill me either. I remember my throat being on fire, but I was still alive. I thought to myself, I can't even kill myself, right?

Though life was depressing, disheartening, discouraging and frustrating, I knew there was something special about me. Maybe I felt this way because my family made me feel like I didn't belong. Whatever the reason, I was determined to persevere; I was determined to win at all costs.

*God will finish whatever he's started in my life.

The moment God put a dream in your heart, and the moment the promise took root, He not only started it, but He set a completion date. God is called the author and the finisher of our faith. He is Alpha and Omega, meaning the beginning and the end. God wouldn't have given you the dream; the promise wouldn't have come alive if God didn't already have a plan to bring it to pass. Doesn't matter how long it's been or how impossible it looks. Your mind may tell you it's too late. You missed too many opportunities. It's never going to happen. No, God is saying it's not over—I have the final say. I've already set the completion date, and if you will stay in faith and not talk yourself out of it, it's just a matter of time before it comes to pass, but some of us have lost our fire. At one time, you believed you could do something great. You had a big dream. Maybe you believed you could start that business, believed that you'd get healthy again, believed that you'd fall in love and get married, but it's been so long. You tried, and it didn't work out. The loan didn't go through. The medical report wasn't good. Now, the "never lies" are playing in your mind, telling you you'll never get well. You'll never get married. You'll never accomplish my dreams. No, you must have a new perspective. The creator of the universe has already set that completion date.

★ Just because it's delayed doesn't mean it's denied

Just because it hasn't happened yet doesn't mean it's not going to happen. God has already lined up the right people, the right breaks, and the right answers. Everything you need is already in your future. Now, you've got to shake off the doubt, shake off the discouragement. Whether it's been a year, five years, or fifty years, what God promised you, he still has every intention of bringing it to pass.

In the scripture **Luke 2:25-26,** there's a man by the name of Simeon. An angel appeared unto him and told him, "You will not die until you see the birth of Christ." You can imagine how far out that promise seemed, especially back then. He would see the birth of the Messiah. Simeon didn't tell anyone about it, he kept it to himself. Do you know, some promises you're not supposed to tell your friends and all your family members? They may not be happy for you. They may tell you how it's not going to happen and you're too old. Do you really think you can do that? Keep it to yourself. That's between you and God. The scripture calls it a secret petition of our heart. A year went by, and Simeon didn't see any sign of the Messiah, for five years, ten years. I'm sure the thoughts came, saying, "You heard God wrong." It's been too long. It's never going to happen. The enemy has no new tricks. He uses the same type of lies on us today: doubt and discouragement. You really think you're going to get well? You saw the medical report. You really think you can accomplish those dreams? You don't have the funds, the connections, or the expertise. No, let those thoughts go in one ear and out the other. I can see Simeon all through the day saying, "God, I know you're a God of completion." You said I wouldn't go to my grave without seeing this promise come to pass, so, Lord, I want to thank you that it's on the way. He got up every morning, believing, expecting, knowing that it would happen, and sure enough, 20 years later, he saw Christ born. The promise came to fulfillment, and God is saying to you tonight what he said to Simeon. You can't die yet. There are too many promises that have not come to pass in your life.

✶ You're Unstoppable because of your Unstoppable God

What God started, he will finish. People can't stop it. Bad breaks can't stop it. Sickness can't stop it. Death can't even stop it. You need to get ready. God is going to complete your incompletions. You will not go to your grave without seeing those dreams come to pass, even the secret petitions of your heart, and it may seem impossible, but remember, our God is all-powerful. He spoke the worlds into existence, and he has you in the palm of his hand. God never created you to do something average, to drag through life unfulfilled, unrewarded. No, he created you to do something amazing. He's put seeds of greatness on the inside. He's whispered things to you in the middle of the night that seem too big, far out, impossible, but God is saying, that was my voice. That's my dream for your life. It's bigger. It's more rewarding. You may not see how it can happen. It may look like it's been too long, but if you'll stay in faith, God can still bring that to pass. He will finish what he started. Two weeks before graduating high school, I gave birth to my first child, who was born with cerebral palsy and is still a quadriplegic to this day. But I was determined to be everything they said I wouldn't be. I left my home of St. Thomas, U.S. Virgin Islands three years after graduating high school in 1990 to seek more skilled, appropriate healthcare for my disabled daughter. I was determined to become someone that I would be proud of. The doctors said my daughter wouldn't live past the age of one. But I'm here to tell you no matter what comes my way, I believe in the promise God made to me. He gave me a vision of my daughter coming up to my bed and tapping me, standing up and walking to my bedside without any assistance. God promised me that I will live to see her walk. I can't die yet because God made me a promise. I can't die until I see God bring every promise to pass.

★ Life may throw curve balls at you, but bob, weave and keep moving

You've got to stir up what God's put on the inside of you. Life will try to push you down, steal your dreams, and talk you into settling for mediocrity, but I want you to have this new attitude. What God started in your life, he is going to finish it, but here's the real question. Will you keep believing even though it looks impossible? Will you stay in faith even though every voice tells you that it's not going to happen? In **1 Samuel chapter 16**, David was anointed to be king at 17 years of age, but he didn't take the throne until he was 30. For 13 years, he had a lot come against him. King Saul was jealous of him, and tried to kill him. Even though David had done no wrong, he had to live on the run, hiding in the caves, year after year, and I'm sure he thought, *God, did I hear you wrong? Is it ever going to happen?*

At one point, a man named Nabal insulted David. He wouldn't give David's men any food, even though they had been protecting his property, and this set David off. He was furious. I don't think so much it was the fact that Nabal was rude, but it was the fact that David had 13 years of pent-up frustration on the inside. He'd heard the voice again and again, "Look at you, man." You're supposed to be a king. You're out here living like a caveman. David and his men set out toward Nabal's property. They were going to wipe him out, but along the way, a young lady showed up by the name of Abigail. This was Nabal's wife. She said, David, you're the next king of Israel. You are destined to take the throne. Why are you going to go mess with my husband? That's like swatting a little fly. She reminded David what God had spoken over him. David said, You know what? You're right. I know there's a promise in me, and I'm not going to let the fact that it's taking a long time cause me to get frustrated and make a poor decision that could hinder my destiny. He turned around and went back home.

✷ Your Purpose is God's Promise

God has put a promise in every one of us, but maybe, like David, right now, you're in the wilderness where you don't see anything happening. You think, I've been praying, believing for a year, five years, ten years. It's never going to work out. No, let me be the voice of Abigail. Stay the course. Keep believing. You may be tired, discouraged, tempted to be frustrated, but don't give up on your future.

Stay on the high road. Our God is a faithful God. It may be taking up a long time, but what he started, he will finish. On this journey called life, there will be times when we will wonder if we heard God right. I remember God saying I will make them out a liar. Don't worry you're rejected now, but you will be celebrated one day and the same ones that rejected you will celebrate you. He brought back the scripture to me: The stone that the builder rejected will be the head corner stone. I promise you it didn't feel like it when I was going through a lack in my finances, going from job to job, opening various kinds of businesses, having serious health issues and living in the hospitals. But, now it makes sense because I can see it, I can feel it, and I'm living it. You have to believe and trust in what you cannot see, even when it doesn't look like it. How many times, as we're believing for what God promised us, do we hear this same type of voices? If you were going to get healed, you'd feel better by now. If you were going to get married, you would have met somebody by now. There will always be voices trying to convince us it's too late. You're going the wrong way. It's never going to happen. But, believe God and not your eyes, your ears or the voices in your head.

✱ Don't focus on the distraction focus on the destination

Sometimes in life, fog will set in. You don't know which way is the right direction. You know God's put a promise in your heart, but every voice tells you it's not going to happen. You're too old. You missed too many opportunities. You don't have the connections. In the foggy times, where you don't see anything happening, that's when you have to dig your heels in and say, God, I'm going to believe what you promised me in spite of how I feel, in spite of what people are telling me, in spite of how it looks. God, I'm going to keep acting like what you said is true. I'm going to keep believing you're on the throne. I know you're a faithful God. What you promised, you will bring to pass. There's a young lady in the scripture by the name of Rachel. She wanted to have a baby so badly. God put this dream in her heart, but year after year went by, and she couldn't conceive. The same time, her sister, Leah, had a baby. Rachel was happy for and congratulated her, but she kept praying all the while; Rachel did believe in her own baby but had no success. Well, Leah had another child, another baby, and another and another, and, of course, it's good to be happy for others. It's good to rejoice with them, but God doesn't want you to just celebrate everybody else. God wants to bring your dreams to pass. God wants to give you the desires of your heart. He wants you to be celebrating, and Rachel did her best to keep praying and believing, but after years of frustration, seeing her sister have babies, her not having a child, she got discouraged and thought, hey, this is my lot in life. It's never going to happen. One thing I love about God is just because we give up on a dream doesn't mean that God gives up on the dream. The scripture says God remembered Rachel. It didn't say that Rachel remembered God. This is how much God wants you to fulfill your destiny. It says God remembered Rachel, answered her prayer, and gave her a baby. God is so loving. He's so merciful. Even when we become too discouraged to believe, God does not forget what he promised us. You may feel like Rachel. Your life hasn't turned out the way you had hoped. You prayed. You believed. You worked hard. You put forth the effort, but it didn't work out. Now, you're kind of thinking, hey, I'm never going to be happy again, never be married, never accomplish my dreams.

✴ Your Destination is derived from your Destiny

No, God not only remembers you, He remembers the promise he put in you. He knows what he's destined for you to do. You may already have said, forget it. It's never going to happen. The good news is you don't have the final say. God has the final say, and He says, what I started in you, that dream you gave up on, God didn't give up on. When I closed my group homes which was my money maker, I truly thought it was the end. I tried many other businesses after that, and they never arose to the success that I had in the group homes. I remember being so ill I could no longer work, and I had to apply for disability. I had to stop working for a period of two years to be approved. It was one of the hardest times of my life. I went from shopping and never looking at prices to being unable to shop or even feed my children at times. During my pity party, God gave me a word and He said you thought you lost clients, but you will have so many clients you can't even care for them all. He proceeded to show me in a vision where I was the owner of this big building like a hospital and inside the building was filled with clients, and there was a sidewalk that went all around the building. I had clients on hospital beds lined up on the sidewalk, and the nurses with their little nursing hats on were walking around the building caring for clients outside. He said you're complaining about what you lost, but I will give you more than you ever had. This vision was shown to me over 15 years ago, and here I am today with so many clients I don't have enough staff that my company had to create a waiting list. What God starts, he will finish. You may not see how it can happen. It may look like you're too old. You missed too many opportunities. It's impossible. No, God has it all figured out. God knows how to connect the dots. Here's the key. God is not okay with you fulfilling half of your destiny. He's not okay with you fulfilling a part of it. God is going to make sure you complete what he put you here to do.

Today, I own home Health Care Agencies in the U.S. Virgin Islands and in Florida. I own Mental Health practices in the U.S. Virgin Islands and in Florida. We are short-staffed in both agencies. God knows how to bring your dreams to pass.

Now, you say, this all sounds good, very encouraging, but you don't know my situation. I think it's too late for me. That's what two sisters in the scripture thought, Mary and Martha. Their brother, Lazarus, was extremely sick. They sent word for their good friend, Jesus, to come to their city and pray for him. A day went by, and Jesus didn't show up. They asked the people they sent, did you tell Jesus it was us? Yes, we told him. Did you explain how sick Lazarus was? We explained it to him. They couldn't understand why Jesus wouldn't come immediately. Lazarus ended up dying. Four days later, Jesus showed up. Mary said, Jesus, if you'd been here sooner, my brother would still be alive. Have you ever felt like God showed up too late? Maybe things would've worked out if he'd just gotten there a little sooner. That's the way they felt. You know how the story ends. Jesus spoke to Lazarus, and he came back to life, but what I want you to see is they wanted Jesus to come and heal their brother, but Jesus wasn't thinking about a healing. He was thinking about a resurrection. A healing would have been good, but Jesus had something better in mind.

* Let go, let God and live in his fullness

When the promise doesn't turn out the way you thought; when it doesn't happen on your timetable, it's easy to get discouraged and to feel like God let you down, but the truth is, that means God has something better in store. You prayed. You worked hard. You believed it, but you didn't get the promotion. The door closed. Don't get discouraged. That would have been a healing. God has a resurrection. Dare to trust him. He's promised what he started in your life, He will finish it. If you'll let God do it his way, it'll always turn out better than you'd ever imagined.

There's a man in the scripture by the name of Zerubbabel. He had a dream to rebuild the temple. The whole city had been destroyed. He came back and laid the foundation, but the people in the city weren't for him. They didn't want the temple rebuilt. They went to the judge, and he issued an order telling him to stop. For ten years, no work was done. I can imagine Zerubbabel week after week, going by the property and seeing the empty foundation, all the supplies stacked up. It's like rubbing salt on a wound. I'm sure he thought, God, I started off good and had big dreams. These people came against me and had so much opposition. He's down, discouraged, thinking that it could never happen, but remember, God never starts something that he can't finish. One day, a prophet by the name of Zachariah showed up and said, Zerubbabel, God sent me all this way to give you two words:

Begin again. Faith shot up in his heart. He said, you mean God can still bring it to pass? Do you realize it's been ten years? Do you know how many people are against me? Do you really think that I can still do it? Zachariah said, "I don't think you can do it. I know you can do it, and God says get started."

★ Begin to believe again and get ready for Breakthrough

God is saying the same thing to each one of us. Begin again. Get your dreams back. Get your hopes up. God has put some kind of promise in your heart. Like him, maybe it's been years. You tried. It didn't work out. You had some setbacks. God is saying it's time to start dreaming again. Start believing again. Start praying again. Start expecting again. Some of you wanted to buy that new house. You didn't qualify for it. It didn't work out. That was ten years ago. God says, begin again. Some of you at one time, you knew you could break that addiction, but it didn't happen. Now, you've gotten comfortable. God is saying, begin again.

Some of you had a big dream for your life. You were going to break out of the mold and set a new standard for your family, but you had some disappointments. Nobody believed in you. Nobody encouraged you. Now, you think it's over, but God is saying it's not over. I have the final say. Begin again. You have seeds of greatness on the inside. God wouldn't have put the promise in your heart unless he already intended to bring to pass. Here's how the scripture puts it in **Philippians 1:6** "Being confident of this: he that began a good work in you will bring it to completion." Friends, God is saying to each of you tonight, I'm going to complete your incompletions. I'm going to finish what I started. I remember the dreams I placed in your heart. I've lined up the right people and the right opportunities. It's not too late. You haven't missed too many opportunities. You haven't made too many mistakes. Begin again. Get your fire back. Get your passion back, and remember, if it doesn't happen your way, keep the right perspective. That would have been a healing. God has a resurrection. He has something better coming your way, and if you'll stir your faith up, like Zerubbabel told Zachariah to be confident that God will finish what he started, then I believe and declare God is going to complete your incompletions. He is going to shift things in your favor. He will release a flood of his goodness, a flood of mercy, and ideas. You will overcome every obstacle, defeat every enemy, and become everything God's created you to be, in Jesus's name.

When you are pregnant with purpose, nothing or no one can stop you. The very trauma that almost killed you will cause you to triumph. Your pain was produced to propel you into your purpose. All the experiences that you thought would break you were necessary to build you. Don't give up; you were created for destiny and purpose.

Dr. Gail James Acknowledgments

I would like to acknowledge my husband, Ricky James Jr.

My children, Kelvin Samuel II, Khristjan Samuel, Abigail Jarvis, and Tyrell James.

Dr. Gail James

Dr. Gail James is a licensed therapist, specializing in trauma, grief, and substance abuse. She's a motivational speaker, international speaker, pastor, best-selling author, entrepreneur, CEO, and domestic violence and childhood sexual abuse advocate. Dr. James is the chairman and founder of Virgin Islands Agency for Restorative Care, Inc., a non-profit organization in the U.S. Virgin Islands that specializes in providing mental health services, parent classes, bullying prevention, group violence intervention and care for the homeless. Dr. James is also the owner and president of Heavenly Home Sweet Home, inc., which is a home health care agencies that provides services in Florida and the U.S. Virgin Islands. Dr. James is a wife and mother. Dr. James though originally from St. Thomas U.S. Virgin Islands, has made the mainland her home since the year 1993. Dr. James earned her Bachelor's Degree in Psychology from Palm Beach State College in 2002. She went on to earn her Master's Degree in Biblical Studies in 2014 and her PhD in Christian Counseling in 2015 from St. Thomas Christian University. Dr. James went on to earn her certification in trauma counseling, grief counseling, and substance abuse from PESI Continuing

Studies in the year 2020. Though Dr. James serves individuals dealing with domestic violence, marital issues, sexual abuse, trauma, substance abuse, mental health, depression, anxiety, and PTSD, just to name a few. Her personal interests focus on encouraging, motivating, uplifting, and mentoring women to assist them in reaching their maximum potential. She does this through her other non-profit organization, Sanctuary of Change, Inc., which provides services for the suppressed, oppressed, and depressed. It is here that Dr. James finds her most joy in providing free services for survivors of domestic violence and sexual abuse. Dr. James is currently a member of the American Counseling Association, the American Association of Pastoral Counselors, the American Association of Pastoral Therapists, and a committee member of the National Small Business Association. Dr. James is passionate about serving God while helping others along with motivating, uplifting, and supporting everyone she comes in contact with!!

Contact Information:

Facebook: Gail K James
Instagram: theRealDrGailJames
Linked In: Dr. Gail K James
Twitter: DrGailJames
Website: therealdrgailjames@gmail.com
Phone: 904-755-6623
ClubHouse: Dr. Gail James

Winnie's Coat of Many Colors

Edwina Wilson

Hello my name is Edwina Wilson and boy, do I have a story for you. My story is one of triumph and heartache, but first and foremost, I am a mother to 4 lovely young adults, 7 grandchildren, and 2 great-grandbabies. And an amazing, loving, caring husband. Mind you, he's my second husband. I know God sent him my way. My Boaz with a twist. He loves everyone and loves my children as if they were his own.

When I was younger, I had a very fulfilled life with my parents giving us many things and my mother keeping us involved in different community activities. I pretty much wanted for nothing. I enjoyed life as a kid, except when my dad was mean. But the one thing I needed the most was love. We didn't have the hugs or I love you from my parents. But they took great care of us. I was raised with 2 sisters and a brother; my oldest sister is deceased. Boy, do I miss her; she was my confidant and best friend. She was the oldest, and I was the second oldest, then my brother and my other sister. We were only a year apart.

I realized my life moving away at a young age was the worst choice I could have made because my life became a living hell. Young and bad choices. Young and not taught about adulting. Young and having no one to tell your most intimate and confidential issues to as a secondary person other than my sister. Young and trying to handle life one step at a time. Young and burying life.

While in school, I worked out of my 11th grade into my senior year at the Library of Congress in Washington, DC, on a COE program the school offered as an elective. I was hoping to get out as fast as I could, hoping it would lead to a better life. I got married at the young age of 17, right out of high school, and moved to Norfolk, VA, to what I thought at the time was the love of my life from the 8th grade, only to find out he had plans with others. For myself, I realized that getting married young wasn't the best choice and my mother told me so as well. I guess today, I can say that's one time I wish I had listened to my mother. Along with marriage challenges, I wasn't at my best. Yes, I became that person that was accused so much that I became her. I went through life working and trying to raise my kids with one who has a disability called cerebral palsy and other challenges with little help most of the time. Life in the first marriage was very challenging for many years, but being young, I didn't know when to stay away and leave it where it was. His being in the military took a major toll on our family in so many different ways that it was not worth being together. But I never walked away and stayed. I attempted a few times, but I went back to what I thought would change but it didn't. Twelve years later, we separated, then divorced after he came from the sea, dating someone else. Life after marriage sent me on a whirlwind of challenges. Caring for 4 children, 1 with a disability, 1 toddler and 1 infant, and my oldest. Mother did everything she could to survive and care for the children. But to God be ALL the Glory He Kept Me and I do me, Through IT ALL.

Many life lessons. Day in and day out, I worked trying to give my children a great life with what I had more than what they wanted. I had so many jobs; some I liked, others I didn't, but I kept on because I needed to care for my children. I also wanted someone to love me and my children, for I couldn't see it any other way until I met the person who would be the helper I needed. Though we went through our own struggles in our relationship, we made it. He cared for my children and always looked at them as his kids, and they loved him for that. I moved to Maryland and for years, I was surrounded by family but felt the most alone I ever felt and boy, it was a struggle. Today, I call it a life of making the wrong decision, which I thought at the time was the best but it was a living hell. On one hand, I had the ex-husband still around and no family love or support, all this while trying to build on my new relationship and navigate through life. One day, I looked up and years had passed by, and my daughter Kelly, who has CP was getting older and I had a lot more to handle alone with my other kids, who were also growing and developing their own opinions and personalities that I had to deal with. All I can say is it was a fight, and I was up against the wall trying to be a supportive mother and a strong woman while also trying to forge my own path. My husband and I talked about returning to the place where it all started, Virginia Beach, and after some deliberation, we decided it was best for us and the kids. Once we moved back, it wasn't all peaches and crème with a short stint of being homeless again and fighting to provide some form of stability for my growing family. One day, I explained to my husband I wanted to start a radio show, and he being the supportive person he is, went to work learning and building what would become a great platform for me to spread my already strong message and advocacy for those with special needs based on the journey with my daughter Kelly. Fast forward, we are now in our 10th year of my Nonprofit and 6 years into the radio station along with online content and having a social media footprint.

The moral of the story is no matter how many times you get knocked down, you can still get up and forge a path with the help of God, who is always on and by your side.

Edwina Wilson Acknowledgements

To my children that withstood and weathered the storm with me and continued to love and stick by me through all my life challenges of striving. Ebony Smith, Kelly Smith, Kenisha Smith and Kelvin Smith Jr., and my husband, who stepped into madness but allowed me to break free without judgement of my past, that's always encouraging me to keep going no matter how difficult it may look.

Edwina Wilson

Edwina Wilson was faced with many hardships that tested every fiber of her being. The 57-year-old mother of 4 lovely young adults, 3 daughters and 1 son, 7 grandchildren, and 1 great-granddaughter resides in the Hampton Roads area of VA, originally from Prince George's County, MD, and has been on a journey of love, resilience, and unwavering faith.

Her second oldest daughter, Kelly, has been the lifeline of Edwina as she continues to care for her due to her having a disability called Cerebral Palsy that comes with other challenges. But Edwina believes with every challenge where she's lacking, she's gained with another. Along with Kelly, her children have been her strength to continue through life. With God's love for her and His everyday Grace and Mercy, it was not easy to give up. Her struggles pushed her to keep going, and one day, she had a dream that became a nonprofit that she still runs since 2014, blessing the community of Caregivers and those with Disabilities.

Edwina Wilson is the Founder of Kelly's Choice Cares; she's been a student at Virginia Bible College since August 2021. She's looking forward to seeing where God takes her on this journey. She's the Founder of Wilson's

Residential since 2012, Founder of The Inclusive Broadcast Network found on Roku TV, where she helps others have their own TV Show, Owner of Disability Broadcast Network, Co-Owner of LetGo Radio Station, where she hosts her own show, Winning with Winnie since 2018 and Kelly's Choice Radio Show since January 2016 where she started at a local station AM1270 in Norfolk, VA.

Edwina has also lived her dreams, being in several movies such as The House of Cards based in Baltimore, MD and others in Richmond, VA. She's played a lead role in Plays where she played the mother, daughter, and announcer for church. And has been in a few commercials based in Richmond, VA.

Edwina's journey had brought her to having a closer relationship with God back in 2001 when she travelled the road of homelessness, living in her car. She continues to believe, have faith, and trust in God, for she doesn't know where her path would have taken her.

Chapter title: Journey to Unshakable Faith

Contact Information

Edwina Wilson, www.edwinawilson.com,
edwinav.wilson@gmail.com
Edwina Wilson (I Am Just Winnie) - FB
Iamjustwinnie1 - IG
Edwina Wilson - @justwinnie1 - Tiktok

An Authentic Coat

Rodney Davis

With so many competing and counterfeit voices, we need the authentic prophetic voice of God. According to the Bible, to prophesy means to speak for God through the power of the Holy Spirit. There are different types of prophecy: the gift of prophecy, the Spirit of prophecy, and the office of a prophet. Although indivisibly involved in prophecy, they are distinguishable in their function. The Spirit of prophecy expresses what God wants to speak to a person or group. The Holy Spirit enables a person to prophesy to communicate or reveal the will of God to others as He did with Jonah and ultimately point them to Christ **(Revelation 19:10)**. Although Jonah had the gift of prophecy, the Spirit moved him to prophesy to Nineveh.

The gift of prophecy is a gift (ability, power) of insight given by the Holy Spirit for the edification, encouragement, and consolation of others **(1 Corinthians 12:7-11; 1 Corinthians 14:3-4; Romans 12:6-8)**. This gift manifests in certain spiritually-charged atmospheres. However, the office of the prophet is those who have been called by God and designated into a leadership position within the Church to guide, give purposeful insight, admonish, reprove, rebuke, and reveal the purpose of God for a person's life and ministry. Their function is to deliver God's word to His People **(Ephesians 4:11-12)**. Old Testament examples include Moses, Elijah,

Isaiah, and Jeremiah, who received continuous prophetic revelation and insight in a leadership capacity.

Not only do we need true prophetic voices, but there must also be unity and balance of the written word of God. Therefore, the proper relationship of believers to God requires obedience to the voice of the Lord and the written Word of God. **Deuteronomy 28:1** says, "And if you faithfully obey the voice of the Lord your God, being careful to do all his commandments that I command you today, the Lord your God will set you high above all the nations of the earth."

As I wrote this chapter, I found myself in a peculiar atmosphere and anointing. My assignment is to prophetically encourage, edify, convict, and console those challenged by grief and your spiritual gift. This prophetic message will comfort you and bring hope during difficult days. We all have difficult days. Personally, my family is coming out of tremendous losses in our life, losing a father and husband, a grandmother, uncles, and cousins, all less than a year apart from each other. In addition, my brother lost two sons within a month apart this year. Another brother suffered a severe stroke. In other words, the cemetery dirt is still fresh.

Consequently, I had the distinct honor but great difficulty of eulogizing some of them. To us, family is everything. Whenever my grandfather had a rebuking, reproving, or encouraging word for us, we listened and obeyed. There was nothing like getting into heated debates about the word of God around the family table with my grandfather. Then there were my fierce and fighting uncles. When we were children, no one could tell us that our uncles were not the toughest guys on the planet, especially my two uncles, Horace, and John B. They were a little on the thuggish side of the tracks but had hearts of gold toward their family and friends. Then, there was the craziest uncle, the "Mighty TC," as some of his friends and children referred to him, but we called him Uncle June-baby. I am trying to understand why because it was nowhere near his name. My Uncle June went by many aliases on the street. Uncle June did not spend time arguing and fighting with people. He threatened you in more severe ways. He and my other uncles designated themselves as the protectors of the family. Nobody dared to mess with the Solomon brothers. However, my uncles had a beautiful side to them as well. For example, they were the most remarkable and funniest people. Uncle Horace is the most giving out of them all. Once, he purchased some Pro-Keds sneakers for me, which I believe started my love of sneakers. Another time, he chased me down the road to give me money to feed my family. To this day, my Uncle Horace slides cash to me for lunch every Sunday. We loved being in their presence. In contrast to their earlier years, my uncles rededicated their lives to the Lord. Sadly a few months ago, I traveled to New Jersey to help get Uncle June's body off the couch where he sat because he unexpectedly died the night before. I eulogized him a week later. Today, only one of the Solomon brothers remains.

Many of you reading this chapter are facing similar circumstances, where those who protected you, gave you godly advice, and helped you navigate treacherous transitions are no longer there to help. Have you told yourself lately, "God, when will the bleeding stop? Will the pain ever go away? Why did you allow this to happen? How can I trust God's plan amid what feels like God's pain? How do you expect me to flow in this prophetic gift when I am frustrated by painful grief?"

Transition and New Beginnings

People often discover who they really are in moments of pain and suffering. Some people turn away from God. In contrast, others turn towards God. However, the spiritual or prophetic eye realizes that God has more pain medication than you have pain. God is the Great Recycler. He knows how to reduce, reuse, and repurpose the pain in life. Whatever is hurting, broken, worn-out, old, and has lost its usefulness, God can renew, revive, reverse, and bring about a new beginning. Do not turn away from God, but stand still and watch God's providence orchestrate the disappointments in your life and override them for good as your life continues to walk in obedience to his call. God will transform your troubles into triumphs. **Joshua 1** exemplifies this truth dynamically and prophetically. In **Joshua 1:2**, God tells Joshua, "Moses my servant is dead. Now therefore arise, go over this Jordan, you and all these people, into the land that I am giving to them, to the people of Israel" (ESV). The expression "Moses, my servant is dead" brings to light the transient nature of life. Nothing in the physical realm remains the same. Everything must change. Therefore, we must be all-present in the "now" and understand that the only constant is change.

Grief and Glory

This verse also represents a significant transition. It marks the end of one era (seen in the death of Moses) and brings the beginning of a new season (entrance into the Promised Land). Endings and beginnings characterize the cycles of life, and we must stand ready to endure and embrace every present adversity. Adversity is an opportunity disguised as a challenge or conflict.

Today, you might be grieving your family member, but understand that this time is not just your grieving season but your glory season. Even while you grieve, God causes you to proceed into the gifting placed on your life by Him. The emphasis of this message suggests that the greatness of your life is determined not by looking at the good but by looking at the grief in your life. In other words, you need no prophetic word to tell you how great you will become because you can look at the suffering God has trusted in you within this season. Grief is often a prerequisite for the glory God brings to your life. That's why Paul said in **Romans 8:18**, "For I consider that the sufferings of this present time are not worth comparing with the glory that is to be revealed to us." One of life's greatest mysteries is how God shapes the heart for greater gifting and leadership capacity in your most difficult moments. Therefore, grief is just an indication of the glory being revealed in you, and you ought to praise God for His transformative power to bring forth glory out of your grief. So, are you willing to go through grief for the glory of the Lord?

Getting Over It To Get Up From It

While Joshua is not generally considered a prophet like Isaiah or Jeremiah, he was the prophetic voice who replaced Moses, also a prophet. Like Moses, Joshua received divine guidance and instruction for the people of God. In **Joshua 1**, God tells this prophetic voice not only was Moses dead but that now he had the responsibility to "get up," gather all the people, and "go over" into the Promised Land. See, you cannot get over it unless you get up from it. In other words, you cannot get over things right if you get up from it wrong. Getting up from a challenging situation is the resilience and resolve to move forward despite setbacks and difficulties. It is recognizing and coming to terms with the distressing reality of the crises, feeling what you feel about it without being critical, and healing as you self-reflect. After self-reflection, resolve to take responsibility to empower yourself and others. Reaffirm your goals or set new ones and go after them. Focusing on your future helps to shift your attention from your past and create a sense of purpose and direction. Holding onto the past threatens personal growth. Embrace the inevitability of change and seize this opportunity to emerge out of grief into the glory of the Lord.

God has plans for His people and purposes to give them hope and a future, even after a significant loss (**Jeremiah 29:11**). For example, at first glance, God seems insensitive when He tells Joshua Moses is dead and to get up and lead the people into the Promised Land. Moses was the most significant person in Israel's life until Joshua was thrust into leadership. Please understand you are in a season where you will possess specific promises without the people and things you thought you needed. God is the source and strength of your life. He has divinely called you.

Incompetent to Lead

Consequently, He empowers people He calls. Some of you feel lost or unsure of your capacity to lead at the next level, but let me encourage you that God constantly moves us to a place where we feel incompetent because the area we were in was too low of a place for us to stay. Our call to a leadership role is different from the secular world's vocation. In the world, you receive constant promotions until you reach a position where your education, training, and experience never taught you to operate in that capacity. That is when you feel inadequate. However, God's promotion is not like that. According to Peter Lillback, your first leadership role begins with your incompetence to be in that position because God wants you to rely on Him to empower and equip you to function in that capacity. **Ephesians 2:10** says, "For we are God's handiwork, created in Christ Jesus to do good works, which God prepared in advance for us to do." In other words, God prepared you for good works, which implies that your call is part of the plan of God, which He equips and guides you to fulfill. You must faithfully and obediently trust God despite the uncertainties ahead, knowing He keeps His promises.

Nurture or Wean

Peter A. Lillback, Saint Peter's Principles: Leadership for Those Who Already Know Their Incompetence. (Phillipsburg New Jersey: P&R Publishing, 2019)

"Moses is dead" means a specific type of relationship has ended. The Lord told me we must discern the relationships we need to nurture and what relationships we need to wean this year. Determine once and for all whether that connection is an asset or a liability in your life. My frat brother, Dr. Doral R. Pulley, concluded in Redefining Relationships for the 21st Century, putting a question mark on all relationships and deciding which relationships get a comma or a period. Pulley says a question mark means that this relationship is up for reevaluation. A comma means that upon consideration and analysis, you have decided to continue the relationship under new terms and agreements because what was needed when you first got together is not what is now required. A period means the relationship is over because it is problematic to where God is taking you.

No Closure

Exegetically, the reason God tells Joshua about the death of Moses is that Moses died alone on the mountain of Nebo. God buried him with no relative or friend there to see him one more time, say goodbye, or pay their last respects, according to **Deuteronomy 34**. They would have never known about Moses's death had God not told Joshua. Consequently, this verse prophetically emphasizes for some of you reading this chapter that God will cause you to continue without closure, without an apology, and without the reconciliation you wanted with fathers, mothers, and other relationships. The enemy wants you to feel sorry for yourself, depressed, and guilty for not getting the closure you wanted, so it hinders you from proceeding to God's promises. God anointed some people just enough to birth you out but not bring you into blessings. Do not get stuck severely grieving over a person you lost; you miss the people you have left that God has appointed to help you emerge and enter into your next season of glory. God told Joshua, "Moses is dead (one person)," now you and the "people" get up and go.

A Future Without Fear

The word of the Lord continued to **Joshua 1:3** that God would give him wherever he set his foot. This pericope underscores the need for perseverance and resilience. It highlights that you will only possess what you pursue, which means that if you are fearful, you have no future. Notice God told Joshua several times what I am about to say to you, "Be strong and courageous." Trust and follow God's word and His voice. To get what

God has for you requires that you walk in faithful obedience to His Word and not disobedience. Delays are often the result of disobedience. What should have taken days took Israel decades to reach the Promised Land. Nevertheless, I decree over your life that as you walk in careful obedience, your season of promise is coming in days, no delays.

Faith and Obedience

God is faithful to those who follow Him. He is the provider. Whenever we are obedient, He orders our steps and equips us with what we need to fulfill His purpose, no matter the complexity and adversity. Trust God to be strong in our incompetency and shortcomings. God wants us to rely on Him in faith. He is committed to guiding us beyond the barriers of our limitations. Know that out of grief comes glory.

Grief Before Glory

Suffering, trials, pressures, and adversity are a natural part of our experience and often precede joy, fulfillment, promise, and the glory of God. When life throws us difficult days of death and tragedy, we must already have a theodicy concerning when bad things happen instead of blaming God and asking God why good things happen to bad people all the time. Consequently, without pain, tragedy, or suffering, people would not care for others.

During grief, people can express and demonstrate soul care for others. Because of our fallen nature, pain is inevitable, but God gave us His communicable attribute of love, which represents compassion and mercy. Ultimately, grief points to the redemptive work of Christ, how Jesus overcame sin, death, and suffering, thereby providing hope and encouragement that grief is not the end of our story. In contrast, God transforms our grief into glory and redemption.

Rodney Davis Acknowledgements:

To God be the glory for things He has done.

I want to thank the visionary of this work, Kishma George, for her direction and leadership. Thank you for heeding the voice of God every time He speaks to you.

"...Write the vision and make it plain ... so that he may run that readeth it." No one ever creates vision alone. God always assigns a team of supportive people. I'm blessed to be surrounded by extraordinary people who continue to add to my life.

My family, from my wife, Mary, and my children—La Shelle, Jenna, Adonijah, Leah, Eden, and Micah— to my mom, Shirley, to all the members of Transformation Church, your support has made all the difference. Without you, there would be no me. I would not be the husband, father, son, and pastor I am today. You all keep my heart singing and my feet dancing!

To the editor who makes it possible for my words to turn out like this.

Rodney Davis

Rodney Davis is a multifaceted individual who wears many hats in his pursuit of making a positive impact on people's lives. As a devoted husband and father of six, he understands the importance of strong family values and is committed to instilling them in both his own family and the community he serves.

Rodney is the esteemed Pastor of Transformation Church, located in Dover, Delaware. With a passion for guiding others towards spiritual transformation, he leads his congregation with love, compassion, and a deep understanding of the Word of God. Through his leadership, Rodney has fostered a vibrant and inclusive community at Transformation Church, where individuals from all walks of life come together to worship, grow, and find purpose.

In addition to his pastoral duties, Rodney is an accomplished educator. He holds a

bachelor's degree from Delaware State University, where he honed his knowledge and skills in the field of education. His dedication to empowering others through learning extends beyond the pulpit, as he actively engages in educational initiatives within his community.

Rodney is also a published author, with his notable work "Designed to Dream," captivating readers with its inspiring message of purpose and destiny. Furthermore, he has co-authored four other books, showcasing his ability to collaborate and share wisdom with others.

The artistic realm is another avenue through which Rodney expresses his creativity and passion. He is an accomplished playwright and actor, having starred in a local production called "Love and Deceit." Through his performances, he captivates audiences and skillfully communicates profound messages of love, truth, and redemption.

Rodney's commitment to personal growth and academic excellence is evident in his pursuit of a master's degree from Regent University. This advanced education will undoubtedly enhance his ability to serve his congregation and community with even greater depth and insight.

To connect with Rodney Davis and learn more about Transformation Church, you can visit the church's website at http://transformationchurchofde.com. Additionally, you can follow him on Instagram at @pastorrldavis, where he shares inspiring messages and updates on upcoming events.

The Colors of My Life: From Darkness to Light

Dr. Jacquelyn Hadnot

As I share my story, I hope that you will walk with me through the layers of sadness that shaped my life. I want you to feel the heaviness of the coat, to understand the profound loneliness of being an orphan with no clear direction. The journey was not an easy one, but it was a journey of resilience, strength, and the eventual emergence of colors that would transform the coat and my life.

In the beginning, my life was like a coat of dark colors, woven from the threads of sadness, depression, rejection, and abuse. Each layer represented a different facet of my pain, and as the years passed, the weight of these colors became almost unbearable.

The first layer was that of sadness, a deep and somber shade that seemed to seep into every fiber of my being. As an orphan, I felt adrift in a world that didn't seem to have a place for me. The absence of parents left a void in my heart, an ache that couldn't be soothed. I yearned for a sense of belonging, but it always felt just out of reach.

Depression, the next layer, was a suffocating hue that wrapped itself around me, stealing the light from my life. It weighed me down, making even the simplest tasks feel like insurmountable mountains. There were days when getting out of bed seemed impossible, and the darkness within me seemed to engulf any glimmer of hope.

Rejection, another layer of the coat, manifested in every corner of my existence. It was as if the world had decided I was unworthy of love, support, or acceptance. Friendships came and went, leaving me feeling abandoned and unwanted. Even when I reached out for help, it felt as though my pleas fell on deaf ears, reinforcing the belief that I was destined to walk this lonely path alone.

And then there was abuse, the darkest and most painful layer of them all. This hue was like a stain that wouldn't fade, the memory of pain etched into my soul. Whether it was physical or emotional, the abuse left scars that ran deep. It shattered any semblance of self-worth, leaving me feeling broken and damaged. There were days when I thought my coat of abuse would suffocate me.

As the years went by, these layers of darkness blended and merged, creating a tapestry of despair that enveloped me. I longed for clarity, for purpose, but it seemed elusive. The weight of the coat became overwhelming, and I wondered if there would ever be relief from its burden. I often wondered if there was any hope for me.

The thread of fear, a dark and suffocating hue, had long entangled itself in the fabric of my life. It would coil around my dreams, whispering doubts and insecurities, smothering my hopes and aspirations for my future. Fear became a relentless adversary, threatening to keep me bound and stagnant, preventing me from pursuing the very things that set my heart ablaze.

Yet, in the midst of this darkness, a glimmer of divine truth began to emerge. I came to realize that God, in His infinite wisdom and love, had not bestowed upon me the spirit of fear. Instead, He had gifted me with something far more powerful—a spirit of courage, love, and a sound mind. With this revelation, the chains of fear began to loosen their grip, and a newfound sense of empowerment surged within me.

From that pivotal moment, I dared to step forward, guided by the assurance that fear was not my destiny. I clung to the promise that I was capable of overcoming any obstacle; that I was meant to embrace the dreams that stirred within me. Armed with God's power, love, and clarity of mind, I found the strength to pursue my aspirations with unwavering determination.

As I journeyed forward, the thread of fear no longer strangled my dreams. Instead, I began to weave a tapestry of resilience, empowered by the knowledge that God's love was a shield against fear's relentless attacks. Every step I took was an act of courage, a testament to the transformative power of faith and trust in a higher purpose.

Though fear still loomed at times, I faced it head-on, knowing that I was not alone in this struggle. With God as my anchor, I weathered the storms, and His light pierced the darkness, illuminating the path ahead. The tapestry of my life now bore hues of triumph and perseverance, each thread representing a moment of fear conquered and dreams pursued.

And so, my dear reader, if fear entangles your dreams and stifles your potential, remember that it is not your destiny. Embrace the truth that you are endowed with God's power, love, and a sound mind, a triumphant trio that can shatter the chains of fear and unlock the doors to your dreams. Take that leap of faith, knowing that you are upheld by a force greater than any fear—a force that guides you toward a future filled with hope, peace, and the fulfillment of your heart's desires. Embrace the beauty of your tapestry, woven with threads of courage and love, and step confidently into the masterpiece of your life.

As I navigated through the layers of darkness, I began to realize that my life was not meant to be defined solely by these oppressive colors. There were tiny threads of hope and resilience woven into the fabric of my existence, even if they seemed almost imperceptible against the backdrop of despair.

One of these threads was the power of imagination. In the depths of my loneliness, I found solace in creating imaginary worlds and characters. These fictional realms became a refuge from the harsh realities of my life, offering a glimmer of light amidst the darkness. Through my imagination, I discovered a unique strength—an ability to find beauty and wonder even in the bleakest of circumstances.

Another thread was the kindness of strangers. While rejection and abandonment had been a recurring theme, there were unexpected moments of compassion that touched my heart. People who saw past the layers of my coat and recognized the worthiness of the person beneath. Simple acts of kindness, like a warm meal or a genuine smile, left an indelible mark on my soul.

As I grew older, I began to seek help for the depression that had been pulling me under for so long. Therapy became a lifeline, offering me the chance to unravel the tangled threads of my past and understand that the abuse I endured was not my fault. It was a long and difficult journey, but gradually, I learned to forgive myself for things I had no control over and to release the weight of guilt and shame I had carried for years.

Despite the progress, the coat of darkness was not easily shed. Its layers were deeply ingrained, and there were times when the old feelings of sadness and rejection resurfaced. But with the support of loved ones and the resilience that had kept me going all these years, I pressed forward.

In my search for purpose and clarity, I embarked on a quest of self-discovery. I tried new hobbies, pursued education, and sought out opportunities for personal growth. Each step I took was like adding a thread of a new color to the coat. While the darkness was still there, these new hues began to weave a transformation pattern.

Throughout this journey, I found that I was not alone. Many others had experienced their own coats of darkness—unique blends of pain, suffering, and resilience. I discovered a community of individuals who had weathered storms and emerged stronger, their coats now adorned with vibrant shades of healing and hope.

As I share this personal narrative, my hope is that you will not only witness the layers of despair but also feel the triumph of perseverance. The journey is ongoing, and the coat of many colors still has dark patches, but it is no longer weighed down solely by sadness and despair. It has become a testament to the strength of the human spirit, the power of God's love, the capacity to heal, and the power of embracing one's unique identity.

In the tapestry of my life, Jesus became the transformative thread that rewove my existence with colors of love, light, and life. As I opened my heart to Him, He gently lifted the heavy coat of sadness and despair from my weary shoulders. His touch was like a warm embrace, and with each stroke, He began to unravel the fabric of my pain.

With tender care, Jesus redressed me in a new coat, one adorned with brilliant and vibrant hues. He painted my world with shades of love, teaching me that I was worthy of His unconditional affection. The darkness that once enshrouded me began to recede, replaced by the radiant light of hope.

Every thread He added symbolized a different facet of healing and renewal. The once frayed and tattered edges of my old coat were trimmed away, and the weight of my burdens was lifted. No longer was I bound by the chains of my past, for Jesus had broken them, granting me newfound freedom.

Sadness gave way to joy as I discovered the beauty of life's song and learned to dance to its rhythm. Weariness transformed into strength, empowering me to face the challenges ahead with resilience and determination. Where weakness once held me captive, Jesus infused me with His power, enabling me to overcome obstacles that once seemed insurmountable.

The colors of my coat became a reflection of His boundless love for me, a love that knew no limits or conditions. Each shade held a story of His grace and mercy, a testament to His presence in my life.

As I embraced this new coat, I realized that I was not alone in my journey. Jesus walked beside me, guiding me through the highs and lows of life. He dried my tears and turned them into tears of joy, showing me that even in moments of pain, His love was a constant source of comfort.

Today, I proudly wear this coat of many colors—a symbol of transformation, grace, and hope. Its hues represent the chapters of my life, each one intricately woven by Jesus's hand. I am no longer defined by the darkness of my past, for His love has illuminated my path and set me on a course of purpose and fulfillment.

The threads of my coat continue to evolve, reflecting the ongoing work of Jesus in my life. And as I move forward, I do so with gratitude and a heart overflowing with love, knowing that I am wrapped in the warmth of His embrace. This coat of many colors is a testament to the power of His love, a love that has not only transformed my life but also continues to guide me toward a future of endless possibilities.

And so, I continue to walk, embracing the many colors of my life—the ones that once weighed me down and the ones that now lift me up. With each step, I weave new threads of courage, love, and acceptance, hoping that one day, the coat will be transformed into a tapestry of beauty and resilience—a reflection of the person I have become despite the layers of darkness that once threatened to define me.

As I look back on the journey that brought me to this point, I am filled with awe and gratitude. The once heavy coat of despair has been replaced by a garment of praise, hope, peace, and healing. *...to give unto them beauty for ashes, the oil of joy for mourning, the garment of praise for the spirit of* *heaviness; that they might be called trees of righteousness, the planting of the Lord, that he might be glorified." -* **Isaiah 61:3 (KJV)**

Jesus, the divine weaver, has taken the broken pieces of my life and masterfully stitched them together with threads of grace. In the tapestry of my existence, I see the intricate patterns of growth and transformation, and I am reminded that there is beauty even in the most unexpected places.

Each color that adorns my coat represents a chapter of my story, a testament to the strength of the human spirit and the power of love to mend what was once torn. The threads of courage that I carefully intertwined have enabled me to face my fears and embrace life's uncertainties with a newfound boldness. Like a brilliant thread of gold, love has woven connections with others, illuminating the darkness with the warmth of compassion and understanding. And the thread of acceptance has allowed me to find peace within myself, embracing every aspect of who I am, imperfections and all.

As I continue this journey, I am reminded that transformation is not a destination but an ongoing process. Just as a skilled artist adds brushstrokes to a masterpiece, life continues to add new colors and dimensions to my coat. With Jesus by my side, I have found comfort in knowing that no matter what challenges lie ahead, I am wrapped in His love and protection.

If you find yourself weighed down by the dark colors of life, know that you are not alone. There is hope for healing and renewal. Embrace the colors that paint the canvas of your being, for they hold the potential to create a breathtaking tapestry of strength and resilience. With each step you take, may you weave threads of courage, love, and acceptance, and may your life be transformed into a masterpiece of beauty and grace. Remember that the coat you wear is a testament to the power of love, and with Jesus as your divine weaver, your story will be one of hope, peace, and healing. *"So, if the Son sets you free, you will be free indeed." -* **John 8:36 (NIV)**

Dr. Jacquie Hadnot's Acknowledgments

To all who will benefit from reading this chapter.

I extend my heartfelt gratitude and appreciation to each one of you. Your willingness to embark on this journey with me and to delve into the depths of my story is both humbling and inspiring. It is my sincerest hope that in sharing my experiences, you have found a connection and resonance that touches your heart.

First and foremost, I offer my deepest acknowledgment to Jesus Christ. He is the divine weaver who took my once heavy coat of darkness and transformed it into a coat of brilliant colors. His unconditional love, grace, and healing touch have been the driving force behind my transformation. Jesus, you have been my constant companion, guiding me through the darkest moments and infusing my life with the light of hope. I am forever indebted to you for the new life you have given me.

To my family and friends, thank you for your unwavering support and understanding throughout this journey. Your love has been a beacon of strength, and your encouragement has lifted me up during the most challenging times. Your belief in me and in the power of Jesus' love has been a source of inspiration.

I extend my appreciation to all those who have played a role in helping me find my voice and in sharing my story with the world. To my mentors, teachers, and counselors, your guidance has been invaluable. To the readers who have offered kind words and encouragement, your feedback has motivated me to continue on this path of healing and growth.

Lastly, I acknowledge each one of you who has walked a similar path of darkness and despair, seeking hope and healing. May you find solace in the knowledge that you are not alone and that there is a God who loves you unconditionally. My deepest prayer is that my story serves as a reminder that there is light beyond the darkness, and that in Jesus Christ, we can find the strength to overcome and emerge victorious.

Dr. Jacquelyn Hadnot

Genuine leadership is found amongst those audacious enough to signal the importance of others to the rest of the world. The compassionate professional Dr. Jacquie Hadnot is trailblazing a path where philanthropy meets world-class ingenuity.

Dr. Jacquie Hadnot is a 20x national and international best-selling author, cleric, entrepreneurial enthusiast, and CEO and Founder of Fragrances by Mallie Boushaye, Mallie Boushaye Essentials, and A Woman of Worth Empowerment Ministries. No stranger to establishing anomalous conglomerates, Dr. Hadnot has enjoyed the flex of sustaining a six-figure manufacturing and retail business without compromising the mandate of her life's core intendment: the will to inspire, empower, and implore people. Reputed for her uncanny ability to shift perspectives, enthuse purpose, and invoke change in diverse clientele, Dr. Jacquie Hadnot remains a highly sought-after proponent in the world of business, ministry, and social purlieus.

Her mantra is simple: Dr. Jacquie is led by a conclusive resolve to help individuals attain the strategies they need to succeed in life because therein lies assured greatness, and that greatness lives in all of humanity.

Dr. Jacquie Hadnot combines unyielding excellence with a sincere regard for education, achievement, and community involvement. She holds a Ph.D in Pastoral Theology, an MA in Leadership and Education, a BA in Theology, and a degree in Accounting and Business Finance. In addition to her propensity for educational acumen, Dr. Jacquie has also attained life, business, and cancer care coaching certifications. Her contributions in vocation, workshop facilitation, and ministerial advancements are awe-inspiring, as she has not only managed to lead in sales and ethics but also in creating quintessential forms of humanitarianism, including support groups and multi-dimensional outreach programs. Dr. Jacquie's serviceability has proven highly prolific, as she was the 2022 recipient of the Joe Biden Presidential Lifetime Achievement Award, easily yielding her as one of the most effective leaders of our time.

Whether she is coaching the masses, empowering entrepreneurs, or overseeing her own television network, Dr. Jacquie Hadnot displays no corroboration in slowing down. When she is not out leaving a lasting impression on the world, she is an asset to her local communal body and a loving member of her family and friendship circles.

Dr. Jacquie Hadnot. Business Strategist. Kingdompreneur. Philanthropist.

Minding Her Mind

Keisha Le'Toy Glass

Philippians 4:6-8 TPT; *Don't be pulled in different directions or worried about a thing. Be saturated in prayer throughout each day, offering your faith-filled requests before God with overflowing gratitude. Tell Him every detail of your life, then God's wonderful peace that transcends human understanding, will guard your heart and mind through Jesus Christ. Keep your thoughts continually fixed on all that is authentic and real, honorable and admirable, beautiful and respectful, pure and holy, merciful and kind. And fasten your thoughts on every glorious work of God, praising Him always.*

Yes, do you believe that there is Power in your thoughts? Do you know that whatever you set your mind to, it will come to pass once you believe? Minding your Mind is keeping a positive mindset and having control over your thoughts. This helps us achieve the goals we set for ourselves, acknowledge our true desires, accept God's truth, and act in Faith. The most imperative thing in minding our minds is arranging time with Abba Father. The word of God speaks that He will keep us in perfect peace, whose mind is stayed on Him because we trust in Him **(Isaiah 26:3)**. There's nothing like God's perfect peace. And once you encounter His perfect peace, you will block anything that may come in the way of it. Minding our minds is being clear, calm, and confident, which will guide us professionally throughout the day, knowing that whatever happens, we can achieve what we set our minds to. It also gives us the advantage of being comfortable in our own skin and not comparing ourselves to others. As well as protecting our minds from our own selves. Sometimes, we can be our own worst enemy. There are 5 ways I've gained an understanding of minding my mind by:

1. Practicing Meditations

2. Speaking Positive affirmations

3. Pausing my mind

4. Preventing negative thoughts and

5. Staying away from Pessimistic People.

But when we find ourselves doing the opposite, it will leave room for doubt to transform our thoughts into negativity and surround us with people who deter us from our dreams. The topic scripture above reminds us that our faith in God along with a daily prayer life, will guard our hearts and minds through Jesus Christ. Laying our dreams and desires before God, with a grateful heart, will open the door to the possibility. We should be very attentive to our thoughts and what we allow to enter our hearts. For as he thinks in his heart, so is he **(Proverbs 23:7)**. Your mind is where your thinking happens. So, what are you thinking about? Are you thinking about the impossible or the possible? Are you reflecting on "It will NEVER happen for me?" or "It WILL happen for me!" I can remember being divorced and desiring to be married again, but my thoughts were so focused on the embarrassment and emptiness I felt inside during the moment. I had to examine my inner thoughts and be reminded that what I say, do, feel, or think, affects my life and the people around me. If my thoughts are negative, my actions will show it, and that energy is forced into the atmosphere. Therefore, I had to rethink on my emotions so that I wouldn't create an element of insecurity for myself and my daughter.

Once I realized the importance of building a strong mind will enhance my Self-Confidence and create a better life and a healthier mindset, I started believing that I am who God says I am and that my dreams and desires are important to God. God's word says, delight yourself also in the Lord, and He shall give you the desires of your heart **(Psalm 37:4)**. God will grant you your desires if you trust Him. Genuinely, I took God at His word and suddenly, my life shifted drastically. This was not an overnight process. It was a conscious decision I made to try God and experience spiritual growth while bonding with Him. Instead of following the crowd, being double-minded and unstable with my ways, I chose to be single-minded and accomplish the goals I laid out for myself. I arranged a Better life. I desired Better, I started speaking Better, and now I am Better. See, I was familiar with Bitter. I knew how being Bitter felt like, and I no longer wanted a Bitter life because it brought displeasure, desperation, and doubt, which was all from the devil. But Better brought Belief, Boldness, and Blessings. This process taught me that a mindset for success requires my thinking to be productive. My thinking had to Be Better.

Know that obstacles will come, but remember that the major key is maintaining our thinking because our actions will determine our response. Minding your mind is developing a place of strength with no fear of knowing that God is our strength, and He will help us. He will hold us steady and keep a firm grip. (Isaiah 41:10).

But let's stop for a moment and think about where we are and our accomplishments. At times, we find ourselves focusing on the failures more than the successes. And when that happens, of course, negativity creeps in, and we look to having a day of distress. I've learned that failures are a part of growth. I became aware of what didn't work and adjusted the volume of the noise around me. During the process, I learned about myself and gained the knowledge I needed to fully understand that what I believe about myself impacts my success. What I believe changes everything. Belief transforms the mind from settling to succeeding. Transition your thinking to the positive. Training yourself to think positively in every situation will build your ownership of a stronger mindset daily. If you persevere and work hard towards your dreams, it will manifest. This is not an overnight process. It takes time to build and overcome the challenges we face in life. So, trust the process and enjoy the new person you're becoming. Just don't be afraid of failing because that's where your growth begins. Leave room to learn from your failures and embrace the mistakes. Stand on God's word and fight the lies with God's promises that are true. Speak what God says about you and voice out loud what you want to happen in your life.

Discern who you should rely on when it comes to revealing your dreams. Have you ever broken the news to a family member or friend you thought would be happy for you, but they tried to talk you out of your dreams? Or they didn't believe it would ever happen, but you stayed on course and followed the path on purpose. You obeyed God and knew what you were called to do even though you went through many challenges, not knowing if you would make it through or not. Joseph believed God would raise him up in leadership. He gained favor from his father and was rewarded with a Coat of Many Colors. Joseph's brothers were jealous and decided to sell him into slavery after initially plotting to have him killed. **Genesis 37:10-11 NKJV,** "So, he told it to his father and his brothers; and his father rebuked him and said to him, "What is this dream that you have dreamed? Shall your mother and I and your brothers indeed come to bow down to the earth before you?" And his brothers envied him, but his father **kept the matter in mind**." Joseph's father Jacob kept the Matter in Mind, meaning he kept thinking about the whole matter even though he rebuked him; Jacob knew and was no stranger to God's promises. He preserved the matter and retained it in his memory. Jacob didn't understand it, but he knew God was all over it. And that made Joseph's brothers even more jealous. This story represents truth and that all things work together for good to those who love God (**Romans 8:28**). Joseph loved God and he persevered in his worst situations.

This story is a life lesson to many of us that "Blessed is the one who perseveres under trial because having stood the test that you will receive the crown of life that the Lord has promised to those who love Him (**James 1:12**).' Keep what God said in mind. Think it. Believe it. Achieve it. Allow me to share five principles that helped me endure the process of minding my mind.

1. **Pray** and build a firm relationship with God and talk to Him about your dreams. He's a faithful God and knows what we desire, but He wants to hear from us.

2. **Plan** by building your own aspirations. Ask yourself, what do you want to achieve in your life? And start seeing yourself where you want to be. I saw myself being married again to the man God chose. It wasn't my choosing this time and because of that, I am married to a man after God's own heart. I began a plan of newness. I wanted a new home, the car of my dreams, and a healthy life full of happiness. And I watched God exceed beyond my imagination. God knew what I needed and wanted and blessed my life with a testimony that I can only tell. God gave me more than what I prayed for and will do the same for you. I kept love in mind, learned how to love God and myself, and prayed for love to find me. I desired and deserved love, and it appeared unexpectedly. If you desire and dream to be married, become what you desire. Meet your qualifications as well as the man of your dreams. Just in case a man is reading this, vice versa.

3. **Prepare** to receive what you prayed for. Be ready. We can make our plans, but the Lord determines our steps (**Proverbs 16.9**).

4. **Position** yourself to receive what God is about to do in your life and adjust your **Posture**. Your posture matters. Why? Because you must

walk like God, and He is about to make it happen for you. Your posture will speak louder than your words because I met my husband at our home church, which has a large congregation. And I asked him why he chose me out of all the women that belong there, he said it was my posture. I'm like what? He said I sat up firmly in my seat, which revealed I wasn't lazy but confident. Remember, your posture matters.

And last but not least, **Persevere** even when it seems impossible. You never know when your next will come, leading you to your greatest success. Just carry on, Sis, with your Better and Blessed self! Blessed is she who has believed that the Lord would fulfill His promises to her **(Luke 1:45)**. I pray this chapter and the entire book help you reach for your future and fulfill your destiny!

Keisha Le'Toy Glass

Keisha Le'Toy Glass is an Author, Mindset Coach, future Podcast Host, and Entrepreneur who is devoted to her God-given purpose. She is also an International Speaker who has traveled around the world and is known for her tenacious spirit of influence. She encourages people to murder procrastination by unleashing from their comfort zone and moving forward with no apologies. Keisha Le'Toy's powerful story is filled with motivation, inspiration, and elevation that will move you to much higher success and a greater future.

Keisha Le'Toy is the COO and Founder of Le'Toy Publishing LLC, and includes Keisha Le'Toy International and Keisha Le'Toy Kollection, her very own clothing and beauty brand with bold accessories. She has co-authored four compilation books with other Women in Ministry around the world called, "Women Who Prevail," "UP Now" - Lessons from Women in Ministry & Business that will propel you to the front of the line NOW!, "Revealed"- I Refuse To Remain A Secret, and last but not least, "Over Due" - Inspirational Stories That Will Push You To Birth Your Dreams, NOW! She birthed books of her own called SINGLE Lane, Overpowering the Signs while being SINGLE, and "I Murdered Procrastination," The

P's to killing the cycle of Procrastination. Keisha Le'Toy has traveled to Nassau, Bahamas and (UAE) Dubai, where she served as a guest speaker and appeared on "Manifest with PM radio show with Pastor Monica Haskell, which aired in Nassau, Bahamas. She appeared in the PM Global Magazine as a featured Author. Along with being featured, she was also graced in the K.I.S.H Magazine as the Top Twenty-four Women Who Win and Top Fifteen Trendsetters On The Move, as well as a special guest on ACTS RADIO in London with Dr. Kishma George and many other radio shows. Keisha Le'Toy has toured around the world, empowering people, especially single women to live the life they've always dreamed of, thriving through past hurts and embracing their journey to healing. She has received a Certificate of Recognition for The Iconic Woman Award and the PreachHER Certificate of Completion, where she served as a Certified Instructor for the H.E.R School of Women in Ministry.

Keisha Le'Toy believes that serving God's people is a privilege, and she's honored to share God through messages of Faith, Freedom, and Love.

Keisha Le'Toy is a member of Full Counsel Metro Church, North Little Rock, Arkansas. Her Pastor is Apostle Silas Johnson. She loves her church and appreciates God for the spiritual growth she has experienced and the wisdom of her leader. Keisha Le'Toy is the wife of Terry Glass Sr. and mother of daughter, Ashlin Ma'ia, with four bonus children and a grandson.

For more information and booking, please email at:

info@KeishaLeToy.net or visit the website at: www.KeishaLeToy.net
Follow on Social Media Platforms:
Facebook: Keisha Le'Toy Glass & Keisha LeToy International
Facebook Community Page for SINGLE Women at: Single Lane
Instagram: Keisha_LeToy
Twitter/X: Keisha LeToy International
YouTube Channel: Keisha Le'Toy Glass

Coated To Conquer

Prophetess Sylvia Castillo

The Birthright

First, the story of Joseph unveils profound messages, which depict the multi-facets of an individual's life of tribulation to triumph. In the early stages of Joseph's life, he was ostracized and rejected. It began when his father Jacob made him a "Coat Of Many Colors." The coat will replicate the birthright of approval and authority from ABBA.

The stigma was marked on Joseph's life because Jacob loved Joseph more than all his children because of his old age. He made him a coat of many colors, which caused rivalry among his siblings. They begin to mark him with the stigma of hatred and jealousy.

The coat Jacob gave Joseph prophetically symbolizes the multi-measure of the dimensions of glory, which will be reflected in his life. The covenant God established with Joseph would be revealed through dreams. The dreams will depict the dispensation of time in which Joseph will become a prominent leader of authority.

The Built -Up

Another level of adversity attacked Joseph. In his innocence of receiving a dream by the Spirit of God, his brothers became envious and jealous. They started building up animosity against their brother. After hearing the dream, they asked, shall you reign over us?

Immediately, Joseph's brothers begin plotting against how to overthrow the dream. They contemplated how to hinder what Heaven had declared. The siblings did not realize the work for the Kingdom of God could not be stopped. Joseph's assignment to build for the Kingdom of God was greater than the build-up of the enemy.

All because of a dream, his brothers built up a plot to destroy his life. This is the epitome of rivalry and rejection. Their plot was proof that he was ostracized and overlooked. The siblings were concocting how to exclude him from the family permanently. They had become jealous of the anointing God mandated over his life.

Bounce-Back

Next, their evil attack by placing Joseph in a pit was created for a pitfall.

Once again, He will bounce back and breakthrough through the power of God.

The coat which is symbolic of the mantle on his life, would grace him to mount up. Joseph will mount up with victory over the pit. The devil meant it for his bad, but God turned it around for his good.

This monumental moment in Joseph's life will be the beginning of many breakthroughs and bounce-back seasons. He is sold into slavery and purchased by Potiphar. Everything he will endure will be a set-up for his next level. Joseph will be tested and tried as he transitions through life.

The mantling and anointing are on the life of Joseph, to leap into his next dimension. Through life's trials, Joseph would be tested and tried. The next phase of life, he enters the home of Potiphar and becomes second in command. Joseph becomes a leader and gains authority over all things in Potiphar's house except his wife.

Oftentimes, when it appears that everything is going well, tragedy strikes again. Joseph has established a friendship of loyalty with Potiphar and promised him that he will remain committed to their covenant. However, it is soon broken when Potiphar's wife lies on Joseph.

Built To Last

Above all, Joesph remained committed to his covenant to God and

Potiphar. Yet, the wife of Potiphar lied about Joseph, but he stayed focused on his future. He did not deviate from his destined purpose. He continued to please God and everywhere Joseph went, God was with him.

Also, the coat of many colors will represent the promises and plans of God, overshadowing the life of Joseph. He was sealed and protected by the

Spirit of God until the day of redemption. God will remember the fulfillment of the dream which he unveiled to Joseph. Every obstacle that attempts to overthrow his destiny will be destroyed.

Moreover, the manifestations and dimensions of glory will bring clarity to his calling as a marketplace leader. His leadership role and high profile as an influencer is increasing. Joseph is maturing and becomes skilled and keen in discernment.

Built to Breakthrough

No doubt, as a young child of seventeen years old, he realizes the rejection from his past is staring him in the face. He overcomes rejection from his siblings and is now able to minister with compassion to Potiphar's wife.

Although she lied on Joseph, he was willing to stand for the truth.

As a result, Joseph is taken to prison for false allegations of Potiphar's wife. This is a major transition in his life. His faith and trust in God were consistent. He is unstoppable, unmovable, and unshakable in every area of his life. Joseph's life is the epitome of one who is built to breakthrough.

Rather than life-shaking Joseph, he shakes up the prison. The Spirit of God is with him wherever he goes. Once he enters the prison, a supernatural shift takes place in the lives of the baker and butler.

Both the butler and baker have dreams, which Joseph interprets. He interpreted the restoring of position to the butler. However, the baker lost his life. Joseph's life is not only built for breakthrough but utilizes the same authority in the lives of others.

The Big Destination

Finally, the place of the prison will become the big destination where deliverance will take place. It will be vital to overcoming the previous pit in Joesph's life. His breaking forth from the pit will be the prevailing power of

God. He utilizes the anointing to unlock and unshackle yokes to set the captives free.

God does something BIG that Joseph had never seen. He uses his gift of interpretation to set him free. He reminds the baker to remember when he is restored to his position. After some time, the King Pharaoh has a dream, and the baker remembers Joseph. They send for Joseph, and he interprets King Pharaoh's dream.

Lastly, the big destination is the beginning and birthing of the final destination. Joseph interprets the dream for King Pharaoh, and he positions him as second in command. The promotion in his life will be the place of upgrade and upscale. He transitions from the prison to the palace.

Joseph receives a prominent position in the royal palace and is given kingdom authority as the marketplace leader. The big destination is the finality, where he will be reconciled with his family. The siblings who wanted to slaughter his life with death will see the full manifestation of truly what the "coat of many colors replicated. Joseph is a type of Christ, and the family will receive restoration and reconciliation. Overall, Joseph pioneered over all principalities. He was "Coated To Conquer."

Prophetess Sylvia Castillo
Acknowledgements:

First and foremost, I give God the glory for the opportunity to be a part of this book collaboration. I thank my amazing husband, Jorge Castillo, and my family. I am forever grateful to my Pastor Dr. Vickers. Also, a big thank you to Dr. Kishma George, who inspires and pushes me to my purpose.

Prophetess Sylvia Castillo

Contact Information:

Website: www.cultivatinginternationalministries.org

Email: sylvia@cultivatinginternationalministries.org

Favor Breaks the Ordinary

Dr. Natasha Bibbins

We hear many people say they have favor, but they still live a life of sadness or disappointment. So, if favor makes you sad, why do so many people want God to grant them favor? The reality is that favor comes from God. Yes, God will put you on someone else's heart to bless you, but still, that FAVOR comes from God. The blessing that appears out of nowhere is not ordinary. When God steps into your situation, you know that He is the only one who can give you those kinds of results. Favor seems to an unbeliever as unfair, but when we are favored by God, favor is always fair.

I recognized favor in my life when I was a little girl; while I was not blessed with a coat of many colors, I was blessed because of people. God allowed me to be set apart for his glory, not understanding why, but I was always surrounded by God-fearing Holy Ghost-filled individuals. As a little girl, I spent a lot of time at my pastor's house babysitting their kids. Not realizing that that was the beginning of God's favor, and it is not ordinary.

The Colors in my Coat Revealed

When God blocks so many things from your life, you can only think about how much God favors you. Instead of looking at your condition or troubles, look at what the Lord is blocking in your life. As I went through my childhood journey, I realized that I was Joseph. I would always preach that I was Joseph because hatred will not stop your divine destination. If God said you will be used to deliver your family, heal your family, and bless your family, believe Him. God is not concerned with where you are today; He is concerned with where you are going. Favor will move you from being the least of them to the best of them. When others see your colors, meaning your favor, do not expect to be loved by everyone. God has already placed you in the heart of those that He is using for your benefit.

Think back at a situation that looked to be damaging to you, but somehow, it worked out with little to almost none of your involvement. Might I remind you that it was the Lord's favor that intervened on your behalf? The Lord works even when you cannot see that He is working. Every time the Lord closes the mouth of the enemy on your situation, the colors in your coat are beginning to show. People who know your story still cannot understand how you made it out of your last situation. My testimony is "it was just a situation, not my story." Do not allow anyone to look at your situation and begin to write your story without knowing that what they see is not worthy to be considered a page in your story. *For I reckon that the sufferings of this present time are not worthy to be compared with the glory which shall be revealed in us* (**Romans 8:18, KJV**).

You are Showing Your Colors

As a young girl, I remember people saying that I was "showing my color." That did not mean that I was showing my favor, but rather, I was doing something that was shameful. When Joseph's father, Jacob, gave Joseph a Coat of Many Colors, he changed the narrative of what "showing your color" meant. Take a second and look at your life for just a second. Sickness was not unto death. Homelessness does not make you lose your mind. The lies could not destroy your character. Being molested does not stop you from loving. Divorce did not stop you from happiness. And losing everything did not stop you from prospering. Again, Jacob changed the narrative of what showing your colors truly meant. Let us deal with how favor shifted your life. It is so easy for us to focus on all the negative and miss the favor that God has given us. I refuse to cover up my colors any longer. If God has granted you favor, you should tell the world about it. Go forth and show your colors.

It was no fault of Joseph that his father loved him more than the other sons. Joseph had no control over being the favorite son and reaping the benefits of being the favorite son. Joseph's story is like many of you; you have no control over being favored by God. Joseph was not only favored by his father but also by God. Do you realize that when you stay in alignment with God's agenda, favor will follow you? You may have been trying to cover up your colors to prevent the people around you from getting upset with you. No matter how much you try to hide it, your colors will still come through. Joseph was showing his colors when he allowed his brothers to hear his dreams. It is important to keep your dreams to yourself when you are a dreamer. Joseph surely learned the hard way that family will love you until they see the favor of God in your life. But Joseph, just like most of us, got so excited that he wanted them to know about his dream. The most important piece of the puzzle is that Joseph never told a lie. Joseph gave his brother a glimpse into his life. What he saw was his reality unfolding.

Think back for a moment to when you started showing your colors. As a child, I remember dreaming that I would be wealthy. I knew that no matter what, I would be a wealthy woman someday. What I was dreaming was not appearing that it was going to be my reality. In the midst of dreaming, the place of "the process" is missing. God allows us to see who we are for us to prepare while in "the process." We could learn so much from the life of Joseph; no matter how bad his life got, he remembered his purpose because he believed God through his dreams. We see our future but never the struggles that we might face while we are on our journey. Joseph did not dream that his brothers would sell him into slavery or that he would be in prison, but he still had enough faith in God to know that what he dreamed was going to come to pass. Although Joseph faced all matters of troubles and disappointments, he never wavered in his faith. Get this, even being caught in a web of lies – he still had God's favor. I will remind you that despite what you are going through right now, you still are being favored. God is still allowing your colors to show through your dark days.

The Favor that Blesses Others

As we go through this life's journey, you must never forget that your favor will bless others. Look at how Joseph went through all that he did but still blessed his siblings and father. God's plans are exactly that: God's plans. Growing up, I always felt that what I dreamed would never manifest in my life. My journey through life, according to man, was nothing close to resembling the favor of God in my life. As someone who loves people and loves seeing others happy, I neglected my own happiness. I have been abused by many. I wish I could say that I was only abused by boyfriends, but that would be a false statement. I was abused by the people that I thought loved me–friends, family, and the church. Yes, all the areas hurt, but there is nothing like being lied on and talked about by people that claim they love God. To love God is to love His people. Jealousy is ruining the church in the same manner that jealousy has ruined families. Joseph's brothers were full of jealousy and rage, all because he was loved by their father.

When God favors you, people will try to destroy you and your character and try to attack your integrity. Although it is hard to see, God still favors you in the middle of the struggle. In each encounter that Joseph had, God still brought him victory. This is exactly what He does in our situations.

God sent me to a particular ministry. I served and worked and was so happy to do so. Never looking for anything more, only to be used by God. Let me tell you something: while you may not know that you are walking in God's favor when you enter any space, you smell just like the favor of God. Although I am working for God, the church begins to become jealous of the anointing of God in my life. They were secret conversations about me

144

where the leader advised no one to deal with me. I would be in leadership meetings and the leader again would try to exalt others by talking about the wonderful things they were doing while ignoring the work that I was doing on a daily basis. I continued to work because I knew that my anointing was not coming from the church but from God. God had me there on assignment. Can I tell you the same applies to you–you are on assignment? Every place that Joseph went, he was still a blessing to the people he met. Just as with every place you go, you become a blessing to others. **Romans 8:31** reminds us that "*If God is for us, who can be against us?*"

Although I have once experienced hurt and rejection from the people in the church, God has certain ones in the church who were seeking a true relationship with the Father and were not going to allow the division to be their portion. No matter how much the devil wishes to cover up your anointing, your true COLORS will still shine through. *When the enemy comes in like a flood the spirit of the Lord will lift up a standard against him* **(Isaiah 59:19)**. We cannot read God's word and not believe that it will manifest. When God lifted up the standard, he held back the enemy. I continued my assignment at the church before I received the release from God. Please read that again; I continued my assignment. Favor will follow you even when you are in the midst of the enemy. God used me to be a blessing to the same people who were trying to destroy me with lies. God allowed me to show my COLORS by giving me the favor to bless even my enemies.

In closing, I encourage you to continue to work while it is day. Do not allow your circumstance to cause you to forfeit what God has for your destiny. Trouble may come, but through our faith, trouble will go, but God's word will remain the same. Every dream that you have dreamed will become your reality. Your dream will remain a dream if you do not have the faith to activate it. Do what Joseph did and activate your dream, and believe that God would do what He showed you. I had to believe that I would be used to help my family, and I was. God showed me preaching and prophesying to my family, and years later, He gave me a vision to start a family prayer call named The Walkers United. All I can say is when God is in it!

Prayer:

God, please allow my words to help restore the faith in your people that would give them the strength to get up and start again. Ensure to them that you are with them. Father, please give them a finisher's anointing. Let them not look at where they are and mistake it for their destiny. God, thank you in advance for surrounding us with the favor that breaks the ordinary. Father, we thank you, and we give you all the glory. In Jesus Name. Amen!

Natasha's Acknowledgements

I would like to first thank God for all that He has done in my life. This is not a cliché because when I think about all the things God has done for me, all the ways He made for me, all the things He protected me from, ALL I can do is Thank Him. I would like to thank my husband and my best friend, Mr. Michael Bibbins, for your patience, support, and unselfish love throughout this entire journey. Thank you for always encouraging me to be better. Your famous words to me are always, "be the best version of you," and for that, I am truly GRATEFUL that God allowed you to be my husband. The Bible says in **Proverbs 18:22 (KJV)**, "Whoso findeth a wife findeth a good thing, and obtaineth favour from the Lord." I thank God for choosing me to be your FAVOR!

I would like to thank my children, William and Wilniqua Battle, who have always been the reason why I strived to overcome all barriers every day. I want to thank my family and my friends for your love and support. Lastly, I would like to thank every person who has supported my ministries through the years. You all will never know how much it means to me to have you in my life. I remember a trusted voice said, "A leader without any followers, would be a woman taking a lonely walk." Thank you all for not allowing me to walk alone. I love you all!

Dr. Natasha Bibbins

Dr. Natasha Bibbins is a God-Fearing woman that loves the Lord and her family. She is a Wife, Mother, Prophet, Pastor, Co-Author, Author, Certified Life & Executive Leadership Coach, Sister, and a Friend. She is the Founder of Natasha Bibbins Ministries Forever Fire Empowerment (501c3), Sisters Empowering Sisters Ministries, The ReCharge Movement (501c3), and Recharge Outreach Ministry.

She is the visionary of The Walker Family Prayer Call, as she believes in the principle that family is her first ministry, as spoken in **1 Timothy 3:5** "If anyone does not know how to manage his own family, how can he take care of God's church."

Natasha also became a Best-Selling Co-Author in 2020 for the Dreamer on the Rise Book, compiled by Dr. Kishma George and again in 2022 for Called to Intercede book. She is also the author of Recharge Empowerment and Journal and God Will Right Your Wrong.

Natasha received an Honorary Doctor of Christian Leadership from the School of the Great Commission Theological Seminary in January 2021.

Professionally, Natasha has a master's degree in management, a bachelor's degree in business management, and an associate degree in business administration. Natasha is currently a student at Liberty University in pursuit of her Doctor of Strategic Leadership degree and a student at Old Dominion University in pursuit of a second Master of Public Administration.

Natasha was honored with two awards, a Servant Leader Award and Walking in Grace Leadership Award in 2022.

Natasha is married to Minister Michael Bibbins and is blessed to have two children, Wilniqua and William, and three bonus children, Michael II, Shenelle, and Pamela. Plus, one granddaughter, Aniya, and one son in love, Harold.

Natasha's favorite scripture is **Romans 8:18**: "For I reckon that the sufferings of this present time are not worthy to be compared to the glory which shall be revealed in us." This scripture reminds her to keep pressing and keep pushing because greatness is right around the corner.

Contact Information

Website: www.natashabibbins.com
Email: admin@natashabibbins.com
Facebook: DrNatasha Bibbins
YouTube: Natasha Bibbins Forever Fire
Clubhouse: Natasha Bibbins
Ministry Phone: 757-652-2245

Favor

Eliyahu Shmuel Ben Yah

We have heard so many clichés, expressions, and ideas, particularly of this topic or subject of **favor** being discussed by the various religious plethora of denominations within the Christian Community and of other faiths as well, such as: "Favor isn't fair," "Grace covers you", "He calls the unqualified", etc. But allow me to show you a different perspective through the lens of a Prophet.

I believe it is fundamentally important to have at least a general (but I encourage you to invest time in having a vast) understanding of definitions and etymology of words to appropriately have access to success and not failure. Remember, your words express your thoughts. Why? Answer: *Words are creative, productive, and directive*.

Positive words can create *atmospheres, opportunities, life, joy, health, peace, favor, and relationships,* but on the other hand, words employed wrong can spell disaster. **Proverbs 18:21** says: **"Mavet Ve'chaim Beyod Lashon"** in **Hebrew** and translated in English as: **"Death and life, lies in the power of your tongue, and you shall eat from its FRUIT** (productive, results.)" Don't like the fruits you eating? Then check your THOUGHTS and WORDS. **WORDS SPOKEN: CREATE + PRODUCE = DIRECTIONS.**

And on many occasions, your negative words can produce residual repetitive cycles, thus creating accidental generational curses!

151

Proverbs says: "Whatever a man THINKS (Thoughts, tolerates and entertains) of himself, so he is (becomes). Proverbs 23:7.

Yes, you become one with your thoughts and words. You become what you think (opinions, perception) of yourself and can't get any further in life till you correct your way of thinking of self.

*Isaiah 26:3 says: "You will hold in complete **peace** שלום (Shalom- Shin Lamed Vav Mem), by the thought which abides (meditate, dwell upon) in you!" Think on what you are thinking about. Therefore, we must deal with our thoughts first and ask ourselves: what are we **thinking? Tolerating and entertaining?** Because whatever you tolerate, you will not change!*

Toleration will NOT only breathe life but grant longevity to circumstances and situations, whether it be in business, relationships, or any vital pertinent thing in your life. *Accountability and responsibility* are a must if we are going to make positive, progressive changes in our lives (paradigm shift) and in others as well. When it comes to words spoken, the scriptures demand from us: Accountability and responsibility.

Matthew 12:36-37 (NOG)
[36] *"I can guarantee that on judgment day people will have to give an account of every careless (**shav in Hebrew**) word they say.*
[37] *By your words you will be declared innocent, or by your words you will be declared guilty."*

Shav (Hebrew) means worthless, without value, without weight in the Spirit or in the natural, unprofitable, selfish, voided of life, vain, lacking consideration, being void of empathy and sympathy, and a strong display of irresponsibility.

You will have **Peace (SHALOM)** שלום by that which abides (dwell, think, meditate, ponder on) in you. What are you believing of yourself today? What is inside and has a hold on you? Your past, perhaps? Unforgiveness?

Bitterness and resentment? Abuse? Abandonment or neglect? Fear of failure or success? Envy or jealousy? Your past shouldn't and does NOT determine your future. **You need PEACE םולש (Shalom)!** The Hebrew word **Shalom םולש in Hebrew Letters are Shin Lamed Vav Mem** and when these letters are put together and pronounced, recited, or spoken into the atmosphere, it means creating a Spiritual force or energy that protects us and annihilates by pursuing to destroy anything chaotic or destructive in our lives. The word **Shalom** םולש is connected and heavily associated with the words **Favor** but also **Blessings (Berachot in Hebrew-Multiplication)**, which means to transfer and transmit an ability in an individual, causing activation and empowerment so that he or she can achieve a goal, assignment, and purpose. **READ Gen. 22:17-19, Deut. 7:12-15, Deut. 30:5 Anything blessed must multiply, expand, and grow, the same with favor, for real, lasting promotion comes from YAHWEH (God) predicated on your obedience and comes with suffering** and hardship. **Remember this: there must be a paradigm shift. READ Romans 8:28, Hebrew 5:8.**

"Your beliefs become your thoughts, your thoughts become your words, your words become your actions, your actions become your habits, your habits, become your values, your values become your destiny." **Gandhi**

The core of your belief (education, influence, environment, and teachings you and I have embraced) system is a vital key that can either determine success or failures. Therefore, I am a **BELIEVER- (BE- LIVE). BE** meaning to embrace, accept and become.

LIVE meaning to walk in your experience of what you have embraced and have accepted of yourself. Stop becoming an enabler of negative thoughts, and do not become a weapon of self-mass destruction by speaking evil or negative words about yourself. Accept good things concerning you by receiving Faith, Power, and Positive-filled words that will catapult you into your next season. Seasons change and nature will testify to this.

Read **Psalm 19:1 KJV:**

The heavens declare the splendor (works) of God; and the firmament show (evidence, results, finished product) his handiwork.

Ecclesiastes 3 KJV

*3 To everything there is a **season**, and a time to every purpose under the heaven:*

My simple definition of the word **destiny** is when the process and preparations (***work, action, effort***) encounter an opportunity. It is not just being at the right place at the right time but **knowing what to do when you find yourself there**. Being equipped. First, work on improving yourself and then work towards short-term and long-term.

Define life and value to decide between wanting immediate or delayed gratification to either abort or fulfill your purpose. Healthy habits produce rewarding results. *PRIORITIES ARE KEY!*

*We live in a society today where we are drowning with much information but lacking wisdom. **Knowledge** is accumulations of facts, not subjective opinions of any sort. **Opinions** are nothing more than feelings (in Hebrew is the word **Kyllah**) or emotions that have not yet been disapproved, and meanwhile, everyone is entitled to their opinions, that is… until disapproved with facts.*

Beliefs and belief systems can't change facts, but facts ought to change beliefs and belief system. Feelings and emotions are good indicators, but poor leaders.

***Understanding** is classifications, organizing and assessing facts to determine where to apply (Emotional, Physical or Spiritual). **Wisdom** is applying facts to become a reality in your life, thus making it a valid experience. What makes you wise is how much you have mastered yourself and live what you preach.*

DIRECTIONS (words are creative, Productive, Directive) happen when words are spoken to and over us, thus offering choices, options, and decisions with directions where to go. **Deception, wrong definitions and negative words** give us a false sense of security by leading us towards the wrong direction. Remember, a lie repeated many times becomes truth to some, which is when deception is at work. **Deception in the Greek** stems from two words: **Planos and Planao. Planao** means to roam away from safety and truth. **Planos** means to lie, seduce, distract, vanity, and entertain to create complacency and produce stagnation, thus making you comfortable in a condition or situation.

In my recent book entitled **B'EZRAT YHWH, I will defeat limited beliefs: Daniel 11:32,** I explained how something good is an enemy of what's better. Complacency should have no place in the life of a believer. In my experience, I have concluded that the closer we walk with *YAHWEH following the teachings of the **MESSIAH YESHUA** as stated in the word, the more it creates awareness and knowledge of our Creator and self. Do you know yourself? Who are you? What defines you?*

The more intimate (**INTIMACY-Into-me-see in Hebrew is devekus**) we are with **YAHWEH (God)**, the more will be the desire to take care of our bodies by eating right and exercising; likewise, our soul and spirit man must improve.

3 John 2 KJV.
*² Beloved, I pray that you may **prosper in all things and be in health**, just as your **soul prospers**.*

Psalm 35:27 KJV
*²⁷ Let them shout for joy, and be glad, that **FAVOR** my righteous cause: yea, let them say continually, Let the Lord be magnified, which hath pleasure in the prosperity of his servant.*

1 John 2:6 KJV
⁶ He that saith he abideth in him (Yeshua) ought himself also so to walk

(Derek in Hebrew), even as he walked.

The word **derek** in Hebrew means *a teaching that will lead you into a lifestyle*. This is what Yeshua said in **John 14:6.**

Are you a student (to attain information voided of any concern of applying anything) or a disciple **(Talmidim in Hebrew)? Disciple** is derived from the word **discipline.** A student with **Greek mentality** simply learns to know or maintain a GPA status and passing grade, but a **Hebrew mentality** learns to apply and live a disciplined lifestyle. **Talmidim** means to live a disciplined lifestyle by imitating a Master: Morally, Spiritually and every aspect of life, including Biblical principles, philosophy, and diet.

John 14:6 NOG
*⁶ **Yeshua** answered him, "I am the way **(derek),** the **truth (Emet),** and the **life -Chai in Hebrew (Torah).** No one goes to the Heavenly Father except through me **(My teaching).***

Torah does not mean **LAW** but teaching and instructions even though it contains the law. Following repetitive information without verification is extremely dangerous and misleading. Therefore, information credibility literacy is not only important but vital for our Spiritual, Emotional, Financial and Physical survival to attain success. What does all this explanation have to do with the topic and title **FAVOR? Answer:** We must have correct definitions and terms of words but, most intently and importantly, awareness and consciousness of the words we speak; if not, they become **meaningless (shav without worth).** We have associated the words **"Grace"** and **"Favor"** as being synonymous and having the same meaning, which is incorrect. And to add insult to injury, we have conjured up an erroneous definition of the terms by cheaply and irresponsibly explaining it away as **Grace** being defined to mean: **"Unmerited Favor." Grace** is a Greek goddess, granddaughter of the Greek god Zeus; the one who interpolated this in Holy Scriptures was Alexander the Great, who championed **"Hellenism",** a system of indoctrination of Greek philosophy, ideals, customs, religion, politics, traditions, and this occurred when the Hebrew Bible was translated from Hebrew to Greek, known today as the Septuagint. According to the Webster dictionary, one of the main definitions of the word grace is an extension granted to pay off a debt or favor. Notice, it is not releasing anyone from their obligations contrary to the modern definition given today of the word grace being defined as "voided of responsibility and accountability." For a deeper explanation of the words **Grace versus Favor,** I fully explain this in my book, **Demonic Doctrine of Grace, Vol. 1 & 2.**

Favor is the word Chen in Hebrew, which means **access granted due to Honor.** Unfortunately, we have been pre-conditioned to think that we will accomplish things in life with little or no effort. Everything in life requires the investment of your participation, effort, time, sacrifice, money and suffering, and this is true in business, family, education, and everything pertinent to life.

Daniel 11:32 KJV

*[32] And such as do wickedly against the covenant shall he corrupt by flatteries: **but the people that do know their God shall be strong (effort) and do exploits.***

2 Peter 1:10 KJV

*[10] Wherefore the rather, brethren, **give diligence** to make your calling and election sure: for if ye do these things, ye shall never fall:*

2 Timothy 2:15 Tree of Life Version

[15] Make every effort to present yourself before God as tried and true, as an unashamed worker cutting a straight path with the word of truth.

James 2:14-26 TLV *[14] What good is it, my brothers, and sisters, if someone says he has faith, but does not have works? Can such faith save him? [15] If a brother or sister is naked and lacks daily food, [16] and one of you says to them, "Go in shalom, keep warm and well fed," but you do not give them what the body needs, what good is that? [17]* ***So also faith, if it does not have works, is dead by itself.***

Look at what **YAHWEH (God)** says to Joshua: **Joshua 1:9 KJV** *[9] Have not I commanded thee? Be strong (**Chazak in Hebrew = Effort**) and of a good courage; be not afraid, neither be thou dismayed: for the Lord thy God is with thee whithersoever thou goest.*

Proverbs 24:10 Wycliffe Bible

[10] If thou hast slid, despairs (thou) in the day of anguish, (for) thy strength shall be made less.

Hebrew Torah believers (Jewish) tend to focus more on the way in which you **PRACTICE and LIVE** in the world than it does analyzing the nature of YHWH. In fact, biblical monotheism is usually called "Ethical Monotheism" because of the very strong linkage of rights acts to the belief in one **ELOHIM (God).** While some religious traditions consider belief alone to be sufficient and adequate, Hebrew believers aren't one of them. To Hebrews, belief is most significant in the light of actions motivated by the belief. Salvation is by faith, but after the experience, we must work out our own salvation. **Matthew 3:8-10, Philippians 2:12, Hebrew 2:2-4.**

Faith and Works

James 2:18-20

…18 But someone will say, "You have faith and I have deeds." Show me your faith without deeds, and I will show you my faith by my deeds. 19 You believe that God is one. Good for you! Even the demons believe that— and shudder. 20 O foolish man, do you want evidence that faith without deeds is worthless?

Lefum Tzaara Agra, in the Hebrew expression,

Literally: As the suffering (pain) so the reward

Idiomatically, Success comes with a price!

We have mistakenly believed (we have been taught) and have been confused with words **"grace", "mercy" and "favor"** and have given them the same meaning and definitions.

Even the great Christian scholars of today have been discussing on how to solve the problem of "Hyper-Grace" Gospel being preached in our pulpits in America and how to bring clarity due to the abuse of the term "Grace" in the assembly of believers worldwide. Grace has been reduced to mean: "Don't do anything because Yeshua did it all", "Once saved, always saved", etc. All these are void of personal responsibility, accountability, and even spiritual oversight. We must realize that there are 3 levels of **Mercy,** and we will attempt to define them briefly. **Mercy** has everything to do with **FAVOR** and no relation with grace.

Chesed: *meaning all-inclusive, (involves everybody), the good, the bad. Manifesting and extending HIS nature of kindness to humanity.*

Matthew 5:45 Names of God Bible
[45] *In this way you show that you are children of your Father in heaven. He makes his sun rise on people whether they are good or evil. He lets rain fall on them whether they are just or unjust.*

Chanan: *This is the level where God gets involved in your personal life due to someone praying and interceding for you. Some of us are living on our mama's and grandmother's prayers. Let's remember Abraham with his nephew Lot and how he was spared because his uncle interceded for him.*

Rachman: *This is the type of mercy that is selective. It's up to HIM.*

Malachi 1:1-2 "I Loved Jacob, but Esau I Hated"

1 This is a divine revelation. **Yahweh** *spoke his word to Israel through Malachi.*

2 "I loved you," says **Yahweh**.

"But you ask, 'How did you love us?'

"Wasn't Esau Jacob's brother?" declares **Yahweh**. *"I loved Jacob, but* **Esau I hated.**

Romans 9:15 Names of God Bible

15 For example, God said to Moses, "I will be kind to anyone I want to. I will be merciful to anyone I want to."

Romans 9:16, 1 John 3:22, John 14:21, Philippians 2:13, John 15:14-16, John 15:9-11, Matthew 21:28-31.

The questions remain: How do I obtain **FAVOR?**

Answers: Proverbs 8:17

17 I love those who love me,

And those who seek me diligently will find me.

Proverbs 8:35 *35 For who find me, find life and shall obtain favor of the Lord.*

Luke 2:52 Names of God Bible

52 **Yeshua** *grew in wisdom and maturity. He gained* **favor from God and people.**

Seek HIS face and not his hand.

Precisely, the **10 commandments** are simply codes of **Honor,** whereas the first 5 commandments pertain towards YAHWEH (G-d) and the remaining 5 towards your fellowman. YESHUA gave a synopsis (summary) of the Ten Commandments.

Matthew 22:37-40 Names of God Bible

[37] *Yeshua answered him, "'Love the Lord your God with all your heart, with all your soul, and with all your mind.'* **(First 5 commandments)** [38] *This is the greatest and most important commandment.* [39] *The second is like it: (meaning equally important) 'Love your neighbor as you love yourself.' (remaining 5)* [40] *All of Moses' Teachings and the Prophets depend on these two commandments."* **(TORAH) No Honor, no access. Tell me who you are honoring, and I will tell you who you have access to.**

Favor is predicated upon your obedience. **Read Deut. 28:1-14**, it speaks volumes of the result and consequences of your obedience. But, from **Deut. 28:15-62** speaks on the consequences of curses you will incur if you disobey. The scripture says that obedience is greater than your sacrifice, but how many are aware that even in your obedience, you will sacrifice someone or something? There is a price to be paid in today's society, where everything is fast-paced and only half explained, which has sucked us into compromise. The beginning of all wisdom is to **FEAR YAHWEH (God).** Make no mistake about it: there is no shortcut or fast track. We must endure trials, rejection, abandonment, scoffing, mockery, humiliation, sadness, despair, discouragements, etc. Remember, **Faith just like Love** that is not tested, can't be trusted. The old mothers in the church used to sing an old hymn: "Put your time in." We don't want to be in the category described in **Matthew 7:21-23**. A manifestation of gifts of the Spirit does not declare the integrity, spirituality or maturity of an individual. The gifts and the call of YAHWEH are irrevocable and given without repentance (Don't have to live a Holy life). God used an Ass in the Bible! We have confused grace with mercy. Grace is used today as a tool or license to sin. Yeshua said: "Be perfect **(Greek. Matureo -Mature)** as our Heavenly FATHER is perfect" **Matthew 5:48**. In **1 Peter 1:16**, it says, **"You shall be holy, for I am holy."** This is a command from God—not a suggestion.

Why would God demand something that is unattainable? To be holy as I am holy–is no small thing.

What Does Be Holy as I Am Holy Mean? Read I John 3:8-24

It means we are called to be like God himself. To pursue holiness with all our hearts. To run hard after God. To put to death the deeds of the flesh and put on righteousness. The Holy Scriptures were written so that they can serve as an example of hope, restoration, and forgiveness, but it was never to use any of the biblical character as a point of reference to justify sin. Don't frustrate God's mercy. HIS mercy is new (renewed) every morning-meaning there are limits. Joseph who was given the **COAT of MANY COLORS** representing nations, influence, affluence, diversity, and adversity but kept his integrity, and therefore he ruled and was second in command in Egypt. You love God? Keep HIS commandments and this is how we obtain favor. **Read 1 John 2:3-6, Rev. 22:11-12, Matthew 7:12-14- Hebrews 6:12** *12 That ye be not slothful, but followers of them who through faith and patience inherit the promises. Choose the path of life!*

How then do we connect the words: Honor, Favor, shalom and blessings? The other Hebrew word for **Blessings** is **Levareja,** which means **To serve, to bow and to kiss.** This was the covenant (**Hebrew -Bri't**) that YAHWEH (God) made with Abraham. **Genesis 12:3** A covenant consist of promises, agreement, and conditions. Below was the covenant. YAHWEH (God) blessed (**Berachot** *to transfer and transmit an ability in an individual, causing activation and empowerment*) **Abram** (exalted father) to **Abraham** (Father of many nations). Anytime God wants to do something significant in your life, HE will change your name, circumstance, circle of friends, region, etc. Have the courage to accept changes.

"I will bless those who bless **(Levareja)** you, And I will **curse (melajek** *-make light, speak evil, dishonors*) him who curses (**aor-** *destroy them*) you; And in you all the families (this applies to you) of the earth shall be blessed."

One definition of **favor: Proverbs 16:7 KJV**

[7] When a man's ways please the Lord, he maketh even his enemies
to be at peace with him.

In simple words: Abraham **(Levareja)** who ever honors, respect, defends you, etc. I, YAHWEH, will **LEVAREJA** (serve, bow and kiss) them. Can you Imagine that? When we pray, God Almighty serves, bows (shows us honor), and kisses us! Let me explain: Jacob was kissed by his father, Isaac. It really doesn't matter what you and I think, Jacob was kissed by his father. Kissing in the Middle East signify a blessing. Apostle Paul said: "Greet one another with a **Holy Kiss.**" This is why precisely YESHUA got upset with Judas and demanded, saying, "Judas, with a kiss, you betray ME?" In other words, you turned a blessing into a curse by sealing it with a kiss. When you feel the Heavenly Father's Presence in reality, it is HIM kissing and loving on you! Now, that's a blessing! It doesn't matter who like you or not. If they are for you or not, if our Heavenly ABBA kissed you, that means you got *HIS FAVOR! Have our Heavenly Abba kissed you today? Stay the course, be faithful, stay prayerful, and consecrated for HIS purposes. Be Perfect (practice makes perfect)—no matter what you struggle with and how many flaws and imperfections you may have, continue to remain in HIS presence. Either prayer takes out sin or sin takes out prayer, but the two can't co-exist! Forgive yourself. You got HIS favor.*

Psalm 2:12 KJV

[12] Kiss the Son, lest he be angry, and ye perish from the way, when his wrath is kindled but a little. Blessed is all they that put their trust in him.

SHALOM SHALOM שׁוֹלְם

Strong's Exhaustive Concordance

Well, favor, friend, great, good health, perfect.

SHALOM {shaw-lome'}; from shalam; safe, i.e. (figuratively) well, happy, friendly; also (abstractly) welfare, i.e. Healthy, prosperity, peace - do, familiar, fare, FAVOR, friend, great, (good) health, (perfect, such as be at) peace(-able, -ably), prosper(-ity, -ous), rest, safe(-ty), salute, welfare, (all is, be) well, wholly.

Sources: Jewish Judaica Encyclopedia
Catholic Encyclopedia
Houston & Katy Public Library

Acknowledgements

I would like to Honor **YAHWEH**, who is the **HEAD and RULER** of my life, first and foremost. Secondary, my family: **Queen Talia**

Children: *Gabriel, Gabrielle, Kaleb Levi, Hope Zion.*

Friends: *Prophet Frankie Diaz & Marlin, Sam Diaz, Moreh (C.O) Zacarias Powell, Deputy Sheriff Barry Curtis, C.O. Kimberly Spears (Kujawa), C.O. Brittany Cook, Bishop Francisco Torres.*

Colleagues: Major Kenneth Harvey

MY Rabbi **Yosef Ben Marques-Rondon- WMEK.org**

Dr. Eliyahu Shmuel Ben Yah

ELIYAHU SHMUEL BEN YAH: A Sephardic Netzarim-Hebraic Rabbi, Radio and T.V. personality, and internet sensation. He is dynamic, highly spirited, charismatic, personable, and anointed, and he is careful to give YHWH all the credit, honor, esteem, and splendor. He is an accomplished Ghost Writer, Author, and Book Publisher of several books. A trailblazer setting standards across the globe, proving to have a real move of the Ruach of **YHWH**. In his pursuit of spiritual excellence, he has obtained two doctorate degrees in **DIVINITY**. He has finished the mandatory **HEBREW STUDIES** from Israel at Israel Bible Center.

Dr. Eliyahu is currently pursuing a doctorate in Philosophy and Psychology. He pursued more in-depth studies by studying at **WMEK,** where he was ordained as a Netzarim Rabbi. Known for his incredible prophetic insight and ministry of deliverance, healing, signs and wonders, Dr. Eliyahu is, without doubt making an impression in the 21st Century.

Though he is **bilingual,** his ministry transcends cultural and denominational barriers, for his passion is seeking the unity of the mystical body of THE MESHIAJ. Has served as an interpreter for former **Rabbi Shaeffer, Pastor Benny Hinn, Steve Brock, Henry Hinn, Ana Maldonado**, just to name a few.

166

A highly sought-after speaker, his ministry has reached countries such as **Japan, San-Salvador, Guam, China, Hawaii, Philippines, London UK, France, ST. Maarten, Puerto Rico, Guatemala, Vietnam, Panama, Colombia, Dominican Republic, Canada, and Cuba,** and still travels extensively nationwide.

Dr. **ELIYAHU** is Founder & President of **ELIYAHU SHMUEL BEN YAH SCHOOL OF THE PROPHET established in 2014. Dr. Eliyahu** has a **Virtual Congregation Eliyahu House of Prayer R.I.O.T. (Righteous Invasion of Torah) via streaming live on various Social Platform.**

Dr. Eliyahu is not only an active voice within the confinements of the ASSEMBLY OF BELIEVERS, but he is also known and listed amongst Politicians. Dr. Eliyahu has received numerous meritorious citations and proclamations from various elected officials in NEW YORK, including the state of DE. Also an active, Certified Chaplain for the State of NY, **currently HPD (Houston) Chaplain and C.O. for TDCJ, where** he serves diligently to make a difference in the lives of citizens.

• **Ruben Diaz, Sr (Former State Senator, NY)** and Pastor, once said, "Rev. Eliyahu is indeed a man of PRAYER and ONE OF THE BEST PREACHERS OF NEW YORK!" Pastor Chano Najera from OKLAHOMA (3,OOO membership, T.V. outreaches and growing) says and has baptized Rev. Eliyahu with the name " Lion of the pulpit."

Publicity is High, but while ministry is important to ELIYAHU SHMUEL BEN YAH, Family is equally important. Eliyahu is a Husband and father of 4, living in the U.S.A.

Contact information

Website: https://esbyah.wixsite.com/esbyah
PWA-Holistic Practitioner: https://directory.pwai.us/katy/holistic-health-providers/eliyahu-shmuel-ben-yah
ESBYAH Music: https://distrokid.com/hyperfollow/esbyah/bless-me
AMAZON: www.amazon.com/author/eliyahushmuel

Social Media

Facebook: https://www.facebook.com/ESBYAH

Instagram: https://www.instagram.com/navi_of_yahweh

Business

ESBYAH DISCOUNT: https://esbyahdiscountelectronics.shop/

E-MAIL: esbyah@gmail.com

Business: (345)645-0431

I was Built for This: I am Predestined

Dr. Victoria Woods

1 Peter 2:9-10 Amp

9 But you are a chosen race, a royal priesthood, a consecrated nation, a [special] people for God's own possession, so that you may proclaim the excellencies [the wonderful deeds and virtues and perfections] of Him who called you out of darkness into His marvelous light. 10 Once you were not a people [at all], but now you are God's people; once you had not received mercy, but now you have received mercy.

Romans 8:29-30 29 Amp

For those whom He foreknew [and loved and chose beforehand], He also predestined to be conformed to the image of His Son [and ultimately share in His complete sanctification], so that He would be the firstborn [the most beloved and honored] among many believers. 30 And those whom He predestined, He also called; and those whom He called, He also justified [declared free of the guilt of sin]; and those whom He justified, He also glorified [raising them to a heavenly dignity].

Why do we, as children of God, see persecution and suffering as a curse or a demise to our purpose and destiny? We need to understand that our trials and tribulations are a blessing to us as we grow in our call and gifting to God. It produces the fruits of the spirit, and we gain greater character and wisdom in God.

2 Timothy 2:12 says, If we suffer, we shall also reign with him: if we deny him, he also will deny us, (KJV). Joseph had a dream that he didn't quite understand in the process of it. He had to mature and grow in his heartache and trials. He was hated and left alone by his jealous brothers but loved and favored by his natural father and his heavenly father. Joseph was made for what he had to go through as a young boy; he didn't understand God's plan for him. But as he grew, he learned to understand his purpose. I have a similar story. I was born into a family that wasn't perfect, but just like most families, it had its dysfunction. At about six years old, I understood but didn't quite understand that I was called, chosen and favored by God.

Many gifts and talents were invested in me, and I understood at the early age of twelve I was built for this. I was predestined for such a time as this. Gifted at a young age, I've seen the dead rise, the sick healed and the oppressed set free. As I grew in my gifts, I realized I had multiple gifts and talents that needed birthing and maturing. I never fit in anywhere and felt alone. I always was called the good girl, my siblings always said I thought I was better than them; that wasn't the case. I just had vision and dreams; as I grew in life, I received that same response from others: Miss Goodie two shoes, or you think you are better than us. Now listen, I didn't come with a silver spoon in my mouth; I came from a one-parent household, living in an apartment. I went through time and years of persecution and rejection, hatred and loneliness. I didn't fit in this world. I didn't understand what was happening. I thought something was wrong with me.

I want to tell every young girl and woman you are built for this; you are a chosen generation, a royal priesthood, God's favorite, and the apple of his eye. The favor of God is upon you; yes, you may be going through a process, a sickness, or a divorce; someone has hurt you or mishandled you or even accused you of something you may not have done. You may have lost something or someone; whatever the situation, know it is for your making; that coat of many colors that you are wearing whether you can see it naturally or spiritually represents something for your destiny. It is the favor of God showing you he is with you and covering you. You must walk and be free from your past and walk in the new; your predestination was already spoken before time. You just have to make it to your destined place. You must understand Satan would love for you to give up on you; yes, I said that… Give up on your destiny and purpose. He wants to cloud your vision that you don't see that you have a destiny and purpose; he doesn't want you to see who you really are. You will transform lives and turn this world upside down when you do. So the devil doesn't want you to see who you really are. It's time to shake yourself, wipe your eyes it's time to pick up that mantle/coat and get to your destiny.

The colors in your mantle have meaning to your destiny. And you are the only one who can get to understand what that is. Don't let the devil snatch your coat/mantle of many colors from you. He has a plan for you to fail, but God has a predestined plan for you to have victory. You got the favor of God with you. I know you have dreams and a vision in life, don't let them die or be snatched away from you. You are still here, "you must get to your destiny and purpose." You were built for this. I always say that I want to leave here empty; I want to do all God has destined me to do. I want to get before the father, and he says, well done.

I want to let you know I felt like giving up, like throwing in the towel, and all alone. I would ask God why is this happening to me, or I used to say what was wrong with me, but I kept hearing Holy Spirit telling me, "You are built for this," it was finished before it even started. If you are called to the ministry or the marketplace or maybe you are a small business owner or an entrepreneur, whatever it is that you are called to do, you can do it. I encourage you today to pick up that mantle of the coat of many colors,

"You are built for this," don't let your dreams die. I prophesy to everyone reading this: You are built for this. Dream again, and get the strength and the stamina to press through your pain, turmoil, and trauma; it's time to let all of the hurt, pain, and disappointment go. Tell the devil he is a liar and he has not won this battle. Your eyes are clear now, no longer dulled by your circumstances and hurt or what you are going through; I speak victory and favor over your life now, In Jesus' Name.

My story of picking up my coat of many colors began when I found out who I really was. I had published my second book, I got past the fears, and got over pleasing others and doing what they wanted me to do. I no longer needed outside validation and began pleasing my Father in heaven, who loves me and who had chosen me to wear this mantle of many colors. It didn't happen overnight; it was a process through life. People around you will not understand what you must do to get to your destiny. I had to pioneer and forerun in the things I had to pursue. I am a wife of 30 years, a mother of three grown children who are entrepreneurs, and a grandmother of a miracle child. It wasn't easy, but I was built for this. I was ordained a prophetess when no others were ordained (they didn't believe in prophetess or women preachers).

I was persecuted, misunderstood, not liked, and rejected. I am now a publisher of many books and an apostolic leader of a church and ministry. I have a non-profit 501 C 3, a school of ministry for the fivefold and those looking to start a business. I am pursuing my doctorate in theology now; listen, it was not easy; some of this I saw in a dream, and some the Lord spoke to me before any of this came to pass. But I had to believe and trust God when I had no one to stand with me or encourage me. It wasn't easy; I had pitfalls, failures, and I had nobody to cheer me on to continue when things got hard or failed, but I kept pushing. I kept growing in the heartache and the pain when people left. I had to believe for myself that I was built for this; it was finished even before it began. I am predestined a royal priesthood; I am a son of God. Just think, if I had given up on me, I would not be here telling you this story. I grew matured and became a seasoned daughter of God. I pray that as you pursue your destiny and purpose, you will find it. "Your Destiny Await you." It's up to you to find it. I dare you to pick up that mantle/coat of many colors; it has destiny written all on it. Remember, you are built for this; it was finished before it even started. You are Destined to Lead.

Dr. Victoria Woods

Dr. Victoria Woods is an Apostolic Leader, Mentor, Licensed Leadership Coach, and Master Life Coach, who is passionate about helping struggling leaders improve their skills and find the confidence they need to cultivate their vision for their business & ministry. Victoria created a program to help people realize their vision and dreams and to help with establishing and exceeding their revenue goals and become Destiny-driven Leaders.

Dr. Victoria Woods has an extensive leadership background in the faith-based arena. She is the Pastor of Kingdom Advancement Ministries Church, a non-profit organization. She is also the founder and CEO of Destined to Lead Enterprises Inc., which is a leadership Academy that helps ministry leaders and business owners to find their call to ministry and business. She is also a Licensed Campus Pastor for KAM School of Ministry, under the umbrella of Life Christian University in Lutz FL.

Dr. Victoria Woods carries an anointing to teach others to break cycles and old mindsets and to tear down barriers in their lives. Through her teachings, God's people are challenged to come out of the box of religion and seek a God that is real and can be found. Dr. Woods truly believes that, "we all have a destiny and purpose that is waiting on us to find it."

Dr. Victoria Woods is the author of several books; some are, "A Prophetic Instructional Manual: A Guide to Advance You in Ministry" and "Your Destiny Awaits You-Find Passion for Your Purpose." A 7-day of awakening your Passion.

CONTACT ME @

Email: destined2lead7@gmail.com
or admin email: madonna.mh@gmail.com
Website: destined2leadenterprises.myshopify.com
Website: https://linktr.ee/destined2lead

The Arrival of the Dawn

Kisha Battle Houston

The arrival of the dawn is so spectacularly beautiful when the hues of pink, purple, and indigo along with hints of the sun kissing and blessing its aural presence. I often wonder how it feels to be wrapped around the bloom of pillowy soft cloudscape as I reach towards the sky. I'm embracing the presence of God. I'm allowing God's love and spiritual blessings to envelope and engulf my entire soul. I feel alive and I feel free. I'm no longer afraid of what lies behind the veil. It no longer bothers me that I'm not perfect and that I'm not without blemish. I am not perfect, ma'am and sirs. I no longer fit on your pedestal. I no longer have to wonder why I can't just be who God intended me to be.

I'm tired of others expecting all but returning little to none. It is exhaustive. The Bible says, "but he that knew not, and did things worthy of stripes, shall be beaten with few stripes. And to whomsoever much is given, of him shall much be required: and to whom they commit much, of him will they ask the more." Luke 12:48

I have arrived at the conclusion that I AM A GIVER. I AM A NURTURER. But I AM A CHILD of GOD first. It's something very sacred when I hear that phrase–I AM A CHILD of GOD. What does it truly mean, though? I mean, we are believers; we say we believe in the word of God, but how can we continue to live in sin and disdain for our entire humanity?

We live in fear; we live in reverse, always attempting to correct the past so that we don't regress our future. What are we doing here? How are we supposed to live in a "bubble" society where any day we could die from an unknown virus? Why God? Why? I know you are asking yourself the same things as me, so do not act like you haven't thought of it.

We must pray for salvation, healing of our land, our homes, and our families. We need to be sacrificial lambs for the Lord God Almighty. We must be ministers of the kingdom of God. We must be fearless in a fearful land whereby we fear much with nothing but death approaching in return. "Who is like unto thee, O Jehovah, among the gods? Who is like thee, glorious in holiness, Fearful in praises, doing wonders? Thou stretched out thy right hand, The earth swallowed them. Thou in thy lovingkindness hast led the people that thou hast redeemed: Thou hast guided them in thy strength to thy holy habitation." Exodus 15:11-13

The arrival of the dawn is the one whom has been set free. "The Spirit of God, the Master, is on me because God anointed me. He sent me to preach good news to the poor, heal the heartbroken, Announce freedom to all captives, pardon all prisoners. God sent me to announce the year of his grace— a celebration of God's destruction of our enemies— and to comfort all who mourn, To care for the needs of all who mourn in Zion, give them bouquets of roses instead of ashes, Messages of joy instead of news of doom, a praising heart instead of a languid spirit. Rename them "Oaks of Righteousness" planted by God to display his glory. They'll rebuild the old ruins, raise a new city out of the wreckage. They'll start over on the ruined cities, take the rubble left behind and make it new. You'll hire outsiders to herd your flocks and foreigners to work your fields, But you'll have the title "Priests of God," honored as ministers of our God. You'll feast on the bounty of nations; you'll bask in their glory. Because you got a double dose of trouble and more than your share of contempt, Your inheritance in the land will be doubled and your joy go on forever." (Isaiah

61:1-7) The arrival of stepping into whom you are meant to be. It's time to step away from what was, who was, and who wasn't in order to take back and fight for your destiny. Climb out of that pit of depression, that pit of self-pity, that pit of guilt: for you are a majestic child of the most high God.

Turn your face to Him. Run your race behind Him, for you are unstoppable in the name of Jesus. Arrive in your authority; arrive in your grace; arrive in humility; arrive in the power of the Holy Ghost; arrive like the dew in the morning. May you rest in His presence, mercy, and grace. Arrive right now in the name of Jesus! Be loosed of anything that does not serve you and does not serve the most high God.

The Lord wants us to abide in Him and be strong and mighty in all things through Christ that strengthens. No matter what anyone has done or believed, rebuked, abandoned, and left us for dead, God has never stopped loving you. God has never stopped forgiving you. God loves you in all of your crooked, straight, prosperous, and dry places.

I give myself permission to let go and release myself from this pain. I see it floating away from my soul as it show's strength that I didn't know I had been given. It reaches out and I remove myself from it as it tries to surround and destroy me. I refuse to let it happen repeatedly and again, but it's not just going to let me stray. I'm moving past it. I'm breaking free. "Say, I pray thee, thou art my sister: that it may be well with me for thy sake; and my soul shall live because of thee." (Genesis 12:13) I'm changing my life and it has not captured me. I'm on my way to a brand-new day, and a brand-new heart; God's making a way. The scripture tells me, "And the angel of the Lord found her by a fountain of water in the wilderness…" (Genesis 16:7) I've got a new home and a new place in Zion. A new place in victory is where I'd rather be. But thanks be to God, which giveth us the victory through our Lord Jesus Christ. (1 Corinthians 15:57)

We must endeavor despite our pain, despite our suffering, despite our pitfalls. We have not been forsaken by any means. No indeed. We must rise up in our coat(s) of many colors to protect our souls, protect our heritage, and defend our right to the land of milk and honey.

I feel His presence. Do you? Feel the warmth kisses and sweet spirit bathe you in overflowing love. Washing with His blood shed on the cross for you and me. We are commanded to love thy neighbor as thy self, to not harm one another and be in sweet communion with our brothers and sisters.

The scripture tells us this, "You desire but do not have, so you kill. You covet but you cannot get what you want, so you quarrel and fight. You do not have because you do not ask God. When you ask, you do not receive, because you ask with wrong motives, that you may spend what you get on your pleasures. You adulterous people, don't you know that friendship with the world means enmity against God? Therefore, anyone who chooses to be a friend of the world becomes an enemy of God. Or do you think without reason that he jealously longs for the spirit he has caused to dwell in us? But he gives us more grace. That is why the Scripture says: "God opposes the proud but shows favor to the humble." Come near to God and he will come near to you. Wash your hands, you sinners, and purify your hearts, you double-minded. Submit yourselves, then, to God. Resist the devil, and he will flee from you. Grieve, mourn, and wail. Change your laughter to mourning and your joy to gloom. Humble yourselves before the Lord, and he will lift you up." (Jas.4.2, Jas.4.3, Jas.4.4, Jas.4.5, Jas.4.6, Jas.4.8, Jas.4.7, Jas.4.9, Jas.4.10 NIV)

Arrive but boast not. God will redeem you in time. Consider compassion, empathy, and unconditional love towards others. There is enough for us all to achieve without sacrificing our souls. Always remember that God gets the glory in all that we do. We are mere vessels to be used as His coat of many colors. Just like the fruits of Spirit, the Lord will surely make room for all of our gifts and talents to co-exist. Be careful not to envy those who look shiny like silver and gold; you may not ever see what's hidden beneath.

Wait on the Lord for your time, trust with your whole heart, and He will deliver you always.

Do not get left behind because you fail to release your emotions and spirit to Christ. Arrive. Even though we are undeserving and so unworthy at times, God is still on the throne, working it out for us in the midst of our pain. If we continue to hold on to our emotional confusion, disorganization, and reluctance, we will never see the righteous path that God has for us. We will never see hope.

Do not get left behind. Arrive. When you see others around you prospering and fulfilling God's manifestation in their lives, and you are still feeling stuck, turn towards your inner conscious and ask yourself: What am I waiting for? What is keeping me from moving forward? It just could be that you have been plagued with emotional and spiritual injustice within yourself, holding on to your past trials, tribulations, struggles, and hardships. We cannot hold on to anything that God has not instructed us to do. We must release it to God and let go of our sin, receive God's unmerited favor and grace so that we can live out our lives more abundantly.

Do not get left behind! Arrive. God is telling us that we are justified by Christ's blood, who died on the cross and saved our wretched souls from indignation and the wrath of God. How much more can Christ do for us? We have been reconciled from brokenness, reconciled from depression, anxiety, anger, fear, and even oppression. We have been made whole, and we shall rejoice exultingly in God's glory and His love for us. We have been resurrected into Christ-like characters, and we have all power in the name of Jesus. So, let the redeemed of the Lord say so today.

We are not a weak people. Yes, we may get down sometimes, we may feel like the world is on our shoulders, and we may feel like we are ashamed of our past and allow it to bind us in emotional sin, but on today, I tell you that God is all-powerful, all-knowing, and righteous in His love and perfection. Do not allow others in your circumstance dictate to you who you are to be and who you are right now. Only God has that authority.

Do you want to be delivered from emotional and spiritual sin? Do you want to be free and healed by Jesus' stripes? Then simply believe. The word of God says that we have been given a free gift of grace and mercy. Release your worries to God today. Allow the Holy Spirit to make you over into a new and right creature in Christ. Know and trust that God has forgiven you already for your sins, and your emotions will only lead you to more hurt and harm if you let them take over you. If you put your trust in God, let Him comfort you, let Him guide you and order your steps, He will heal you of all your iniquities and affliction of mind, body, and soul. Be strengthened today, children of God. Do not get left behind. Open up your heart today and release that man, woman, child, mother, father, supervisor, former colleague, pastor, sister, best friend, or ex-husband that has caused you pain.

Whatever you are holding on to will get you left behind. Let it go, release it, and replace it with the love of God. Ask God to strengthen your mind, heal your Spirit, and draw you nearer to Him. Imagine yourself releasing all of your emotional stress to the heavens and watch it fall and disintegrate like raindrops on your face. **Col. 1:13** says, "I am delivered from the power of darkness and translated into the kingdom of God's dear Son."

Go into the light of God and seek His face. Commune with His Holy reverence and power. I ask of you today to let your light shine as a witness to God's love and kindness. You can be made whole again. I'm not going to be left behind. Will you?

Kisha Battle Houston Acknowledgments

I give honor and acknowledgement to my Lord and Savior, Jesus Christ, who is the head of my life, my Yahweh, Jehovah Jireh, Jehovah Nissi, and my joy. I thank and appreciate my husband, Paul "Pep" Houston, for his love, support, and encouragement throughout this journey of enlightenment through my writings. I thank Dr. Kishma George for the opportunity to contribute to the "Coat of Many Colors" book project. My prayers and congratulations to all of the authors in this anointed compilation.

Kisha Battle Houston

Kisha was inspired at an early age to pen short stories, essays, and poetry in elementary school, often winning class and schoolwide contests. She continued throughout high school writing poetry into college as she self-published her first book of poetry in 1995. From there, Kisha developed a love for writing self-help books to help teens, young adults, women, and men. Often hosting free self-esteem and self-image seminars in the community. Fast forward to her most recent memoir about exceeding beyond expectations and generational strongholds, Kisha Battle Houston is even more passionate about empowering the community in learning how to accept oneself, love unconditionally, and heal from past trauma in relationships.

Entrepreneur, #1 bestselling Author, Wife, Mom, and Motivational Speaker, Min. Kisha Battle Houston, also professionally known as Mrs. Success Coach, is a Certified Life, Relationship Expert & Marriage Mentor Coach alongside her husband, Paul "Pep" Houston of Relationships Matter International, https://www.relationshipsmatterintl.com, in Baltimore, Maryland. Kisha has recently received a certification in Mental Health Coaching from Light University. She is a member of the American Association of Christian

Counselors. She has earned a BA in Communications and a MBA in Digital Entrepreneurship and is an Ordained Minister. Kisha Battle Houston has published over a dozen books and resources to empower individuals in their unique personality, passion, and purpose toward success. Her personal testimony is her signature book, "Succeed Anyway". Her most notable accomplishment is being featured in Essence Magazine on "How to Dress for Success" in the workplace.

Contact Information

Min. Kisha Battle Houston, MBA, CLC
Web: https://www.wellness-with-kish.com
Email: info@wellness-with-kish.com
Social Media: @kishabattlehouston @wellnesswthkish

Leading Change a Spiritual Path Vision

Dr. Amicitia Maloon Gibson

Dreamers Are Empowered Change Leaders

*A*re you ready for change? The assumption is that change is inevitable, and with change, you will encounter resistance. Whatever the situation, you will have the *"Who Move My Cheese"* whiners or the "Forward" cheerleaders. Whatever change you encounter, there will be various levels, stages, and intensity of resistance. Resistance is good at times as it stretches you to do a detailed analysis and validate that change is needed in the situation. Feedback helps you to redefine the need and inculcate suggestions that will facilitate the change. To move forward, what is for sure is that you must have a vision and plan to begin the process. Thomas Edison developed a plan for his ideas and a backup plan to market the product and was successful. Not all changes result in positive outcomes. Some changes fail as a result of ineffective marketing of the change or product. Steve Job and Bill Gates both changed the way society and the world interacts with technology. For sure, criticism and naysayers were along their paths. However, many welcome the change, and the results are iPhones and iPads. These are easier changes that we can relate to in the world. The change this chapter addresses will look at the spiritual impacts of change as it relates to family, career and preparing for change from a spiritual perspective using a methodology from my Vision Booklet, *Defining Your Destiny, Are You Ready For Change.*" As you pursue to implement change and it is embraced fast with least resistance, then maybe nothing really changed, just welcome the change and move forward.

Write the Vision

A. **Focus of the Message:** In order to fulfill the vision God has for your life, it is imperative you understand it and write it down so you will run with it.

B. **Introduction:** Empowerment moments of destiny lie ahead in God's redemptive plan for you. These events with destiny will change your life, but they will only come in the fullness of time.

EXAMPLE: Moses lived the early years of his life in pleasure and ease. Then, one day, he caught a glimpse of his destiny. He saw he was to be the deliverer of the children of Israel out of bondage in Egypt. Moses stepped out in his own timing and ended up a murderer and spent forty years on the backside of the desert. In the fullness of time, however, that role of deliverer came to pass.

You can use your faith to appropriate promises that are yours through redemption (e.g., healing, prosperity, and deliverance). But understand there are things that will be revealed to you by the Holy Spirit that are specific to your calling and are for an appointed time.

The basic understanding of your destiny as a believer will be found in the Bible. The Bible is a revelation to all believers for all time. The Holy Spirit will reveal the specifics of your life to you. God doesn't want you to be caught by surprise when moments of destiny come.

This is why He has given you the promise of the Holy Spirit. The Holy Spirit's primary role is that of revelation. The Holy

Spirit will reveal to you the plans of your calling and then lead you through the doors that will make those plans come to pass. You must have a vision for your life and that vision will be imparted to you either by the Word of God or by the Holy Spirit.

Bible revelation + Holy Spirit revelation = VISION

C. The Purpose of Vision

Vision – Hope – Expectation: three synonymous terms

(Hope = confident expectation)

1. The first purpose for vision (hope) is to provide a blueprint for your faith to put substance to.

    Hebrews 11:1, *"Now faith is the substance of things hoped for, the evidence of things not seen."*

2. The second purpose of vision is to be the anchor of your soul.

    Hebrews 6:19, *This hope we have as an anchor of our soul. Your hope or your vision is a stabilizer to help you stay steadfast during life's storms.*

3. The third purpose of vision is to determine the outcome of your life experience.

    Jeremiah 29:11, *"For I know the thoughts that I think toward you, saith the Lord, thoughts of peace, and not of evil, to give you an expected end."*

Whatever *end* you experience is the *end* you expected. **Proverbs 23:18 says** ... *your expectation will not be cut off.* Your view of what the future holds for you determines your outcome in life. What are your expectations based on? If you're like most people, it is based on circumstances, past experience and hearsay. Without cultivating a godly vision for your life based on the Word, you will experience death. Death is not necessarily something that happens instantly; rather, it is a gradual progression. The Bible says what brings you down this road of death is a lack of vision.

D. Write the vision:

> **Habakkuk 2:2, 3** … *Write the vision and make it plain on tables, that he may run that readeth it. For the vision is yet for an appointed time, but at the end it shall speak, and not lie: though it **tarry,** wait for it; because it will surely come, it will not **tarry.***

It is imperative you write the vision down. The Bible makes it clear that without the vision being written down, you will not be able to run with it. Verse three tells us the vision is for an appointed time, which is why it is important for you to do verse two and write it out. It is possible to miss a divine appointment with destiny. But if you do, you can be assured God can bring it back to you. Once your divine appointment has come into the fullness of time, you can now appropriate it by faith.

SCRIPTURAL ILLUSTRATION: Moses, David and the apostle Paul are all regarded as great men of God because they wrote so many books of the Bible. Is it possible, however, that because they wrote so many books of the Bible, they became great?

E. Conclusion: Four things you need to do with the vision for your life:

1. Understand it

2. Write it, make it plain

3. Read it on a daily basis

4. Run with it

Dreamers are Empowered Leaders

*"Where much is given much is required; and in all your getting
of wisdom, get understanding and seek to be understood!"*
~ Dr Amicitia (Cita) Maloon-Gibson

Empowerment Now!

After you've discovered your inner vision, how do you take the next step
to empower yourself to act on your vision? This requires work and a bit
of risk because to really empower yourself, you need to deal with some of
the barriers that have held you back. Build on the work you've done in
discovery and set some goals for yourself based on your inner vision.

1. Begin by writing your goals down on paper. You don't need to share
   them with anyone, so the format is unimportant. I like to collect photos
   that help me visualize my goals and keep them in a folder.

2. Practice visualizing your dreams. If you're having trouble with
   visualization, start with a simple exercise. Close your eyes and visualize
   your favorite dinner. Where are you? Maybe you're at your favorite
   restaurant. Can you see the food on your plate? Use all of your senses.
   Imagine the taste and the smell, and hear the sounds. Repeat this
   exercise and then move to something more complex.

3. Examine yourself carefully and critically, but not negatively. Consciously
   release any negativity that might be blocking you from achieving your
   goals. Forgive anyone who needs to be forgiven. If someone has hurt
   you, consider whether speaking with the person would be helpful.
   Consider writing a letter to the person. You might choose to tear the
   letter up after you write it, or you may choose to mail it. Think about
   this very carefully before you decide what to do. You don't want to
   create any negativity in anyone's life; the key here is to break down
   any barriers that might have been holding you back. You are moving
   forward instead of dwelling on the past.

4. Acknowledge your mistakes and move forward. Forgiving yourself is sometimes the most difficult thing to do. If only I had...If only I could have...I should have...These are all regrets that we need to forgive, bury, and move forward.

5. Examine the connections you have with people around you.

6. Venture out and try something new. Read a different genre of book or maybe go somewhere you've never been. Just do something different. Celebrate your bravery for stepping out.

7. Continue with your journaling. You might want to go back and look at your earliest entries and celebrate your growth towards finding and tapping into your inner vision.

Each of these steps works together and will help you break through the barriers that might have been holding you back. Just as if you were going on a long road trip, you would map out your route; tapping into your inner vision will help you develop the strength and courage to find your way to achieve your goals. Stay in tune with your authentic self by acknowledging your strengths and weaknesses, forgiving others, and remaining connected to your inner self.

Quotes: God First, Family Second and Everyone else takes a number. Dr Cita

Resources

Here are some of my favorite resources:

-A New Kind of Diversity by Dr Tim Elmore.

-Joy Unspeakable, A Spiritual Jambalaya by Dr Amicitia Maloon Gibson

-Find your Best Inside by Dr Madeline Ann Lewis

Conclusion

I wish you great success on your journey. As you discover your inner vision and make a deep and meaningful connection with its energy and strength, you will find increased satisfaction with your life and your connections. I speak to you peace and happiness, and may all your inner visions manifest.

Amicitia (Dr Cita) Maloon-Gibson

Speaker, Trainer & Executive Consulta

www.EmpowermentDoc.com

http://www.johncmaxwellgroup.com/amicitiamaloongibson

Leadership Education & Empowerment Advancement Development

http://WWW.inspireleadgrow.com

About Dr. Amicitia (Cita) Naloon-Gibson

Amicitia (Cita) Gibson, Ph.D, is the Founder & President of MGAA Professional Development Institute and ATIC & MG Center for Excellence 501c3 (non-profit). She has dedicated her career to developing others in a plethora of diverse industries. An expert advocate of selecting and developing talent for leadership and business success who has held various leadership roles in industries such as non-profit and for-profits on board of directors in corporations, ministries, state, local, Department of Defense and federal governments in the U.S. and international. She is a retired Executive Leader with decades of excellence in careers. A retired Army Lieutenant Colonel (Engineer Regiment) with 29 years of honorable and distinguished service to the nation with many Medals and Ribbons. She has worked in various leadership positions throughout the Department of Defense with many distinguished civilian medals in the Federal Civilian Government. She was recently honored as a Woman of Excellence and a Woman Making a Difference in her community. Her experiences are inclusive of local and national board of directors. A Professional Women Network Member for more than a decade as an Advisory Board Member.

She is a Certified John Maxwell Team Member, Executive Leadership, National Speakers Association Member, Society of Human Resource Management, Association of Training Development Member, to name a few. Alumni of Webster University, Cornell University, Federal Executive Institute. Certified eSpeaker Presenter 2021-2024. Diversity, Equity & Inclusion in the Workplace Certificate, USF 2021. Evangelism Certification and Growth Seminar, 2022.

Her MISSION is preparing the Next Generation of Leaders to become the Best Leaders and Executives possible. She says, "Living is a part of giving and leaving a Legacy for the next Generation of Leaders." Additionally, she is a Servant Leader and founder of EWordSanctuary and outreach ministry helping others with feeding and clothing the homeless (Veteran Women & Children). She was ordained in 2005 by the late Bishop Thomas Solomon, St. Roberts, Mo, and received an Honorary, Doctor of Divinity, CICA International University & Seminary. A graduate of God's Leading Ladies, 2007 TPH Dallas, Texas. Kingdom School of Ministry History Maker, Dr Cindy Trimm Ministries International. In summary, she is a King's Daughter, heir to the Kingdom of God. Adding value to others, growing and empowering future leaders now for success. Offering transformational coaching to impact lives to increase performance, productivity, processes and human capital/talents. Closing the leadership lack by mentoring others and giving Professional and Personal Development services for next-level greatness. Empowering others to shift from best to Better and from great to Greater Now! Psalm 121 & 23 are a couple of her favorites.

Chase that Dream!

Dr. Sharon O. Simon

"Now Israel loved Joseph more than all his children, because he was the son of his old age: and he made him a coat of many colours. And when his brethren saw that their father loved him more than all his brethren, they hated him, and could not speak peaceably unto him.

Genesis 37:3-4 (KJV)

Do you remember your dreams? Everyone has dreams and visions; those dreams and visions are desires that we want to accomplish to fulfill a purpose in our lives. Whether our dreams and visions are deferred, shattered, or fulfilled, or whether it is insignificant or magnificent, that dream could have been something in the past or at the moment; those dreams were meant for us to live a life full of success. **Genesis 37** tells the story of a dreamer, and I am referring to him as a dreamer because he had dreams, whose name was Joseph, and was reprimanded by his own father, Jacob, because of his dreams. Joseph was then betrayed by his siblings; his own brothers, and was deceptively indicted and put into prison for a crime he did not commit. However, because of the plans and purpose of God upon Joseph's life, the trials he endured did not stop the fulfillment of the dreams he had.

Joseph had an elaborate embroidered coat. It was a colorful coat, and they were vibrant colors too. The coat was a special gift given to him by his father, Jacob, because he favored and loved him. According to research, "colors and emotions are two individual factors in our lives. It is possible that emotions and colors are connected because many individuals can connect a color to an emotion and an emotion to a color" (West, B., 2019). Psychologists also say that colors stimulate the mind and are intricately connected to emotions. Depending on how the colors are used, it can cause a psychological effect that can evoke different emotions. Some colors can make us feel happy or sad; we can even feel relaxed or even hungry. The two colors that I gravitate to are yellow and green. It is said that yellow is the most energetic of all the colors because it is associated with laughter and hopefulness, and it represents sunshine. Green symbolizes health, healing, courage, new beginnings, and wealth. As Christians, we were taught that once we walk in the will of God, our lives would be full of joy, laughter, and hope; we will have good health, wealth and success and be courageous at all times.

My father gave me a special gift, too, just as Joseph's father gave him a gift. As a matter of fact, we all received a gift from our Heavenly Father; the way we wear our gifts might cause us to be in uncomfortable situations like Joseph. The gift I received was a special gift because as I reflected upon my life, seeing where the Lord has brought me from, I can honestly say that I, Sharon, was favored by my father. Though my coat was not an actual coat per se, the vibrant colors of my coat caused me to believe that color does stimulate the mind and that colors are intricately connected to emotions and evoke different emotions.

We can clearly see that Joseph's gift was the basis for what he went through. And likewise, our gifts caused some of the unpleasant experiences that you and I both went through, and emotions were evoked. Because it was perceived by others that the hands of the Lord were upon our lives, seemingly, they saw that we were favored by God and were not happy. I have heard this phrase several times that "some people cannot be excited for other's future." It is always an 'I,' one can see or even hear that selfish or envious behavior with which you are faced. "It should have been me, why her," "but she is not even qualified for that position or that job," "really, he married her" or "she got what, married? Wow!" Do I need to go on? It is obvious what God is doing for you is clearly in the open; they can see that God favors you, and it is causing discomfort for those around you.

I think you should consider yourself as Joseph because of the dreamer in you. We are dreamers; we receive precise information about our future in dreams, and no one has to tell us, God gives us our directions, and sometimes we become so excited, or I can say maybe because we are not discerning enough that we think we must share every detail of our visions, or our dreams of our future with others. We cannot be still for a moment, "Oh, let me call her and tell her this dream," and with that same zeal, you made that call. And the people we share our dreams with are our trusted enemies, the ones we call our friends, or it could be our sisters, brothers, neighbors, or someone we hold as a confidant. Unknowingly, our future is exposed by our own doing, and at times, we sure will find it out the hard way that's when our dreams don't come through. Now, don't go blaming the devil; he had nothing to do with it this time. Maybe the devil was trying to shut your mouth, and you rebuked him. I've learned that it is a good suggestion that instead of sharing our visions and dreams, we should write them down; if you are becoming anxious about that idea, yes, don't get too impulsive to think I have to get it off my mind, I must tell someone. Listen, not everyone holds your best interest at heart.

I can testify to that; my dream was deferred, and I am using the word deferred because I do believe it can come to life again once I'm within the right environment. I had this burning desire to be a caregiver of young ladies that are less fortunate than others and aid in providing them with their foundation educational needs with the hope they will be able to secure a career they so desire. This was just an idea I had, but each time I went to South America, the idea would resurface. So, I decided to have a discussion with one of my friends, and she was a close friend, someone I trusted. I had envisioned the building, the girls who would be in my care, and a program was mapped out for the girl's educational path. This vision manifested to the point where I was introduced to someone over lunch to acquire a property to establish the home. During our three-hour lunch, I noticed my friend became incredibly quiet with minimal input to the conversation; her phone suddenly became the center of her attention. And I dismissed those actions passively. But words can build you or break you, or it can distract you from your path. All of a sudden, she said laughingly, "Don't waste your time with that; you have your own nieces you can attend to; what good do you think would come out from this, and who would waste their time taking care of children? They could be troublesome. Girl Sharon, think about something else." Oh wait, this was the same person I shared my vision with; we talked about it for months, the same person who had encouraged and supported my vision. It was that same friend whose husband had arranged the lunch we had. I was confused about why the sudden change after working with me for months or whether she was working for or against me. That was my dessert. Her words still lingers 5 years later. In Joseph's situation, his own brothers and even his father criticized his dream.

"Soon Joseph had another dream, and again he told his brothers about it. "Listen, I have had another dream," he said. "The sun, moon, and eleven stars bowed low before me!" This time he told the dream to his father as well as to his brothers, but his father scolded him. "What kind of dream is that?" he asked. "Will your mother and I and your brothers actually come and bow to the grown before you?" **Genesis 37:9-10 (NLT)**

Your situation may be different; you may have experienced a similar situation as Joseph or are experiencing a similar situation. Or you are doing a self-evaluation of your environment. You feel that something is wrong with you because it seems whenever you go somewhere, you are always getting into conflict with others, your family members, and coworkers. Though you have tried your best to avoid these unpleasant situations, somehow things do not go right; it seems to be chaotic when you are around. That meeting at work did not turn out the way it should after you asked that relevant question pertaining to the project you are working on. Then, at the women's meeting, the moment you entered there was chaos. Now, you may be wondering why every time you open your mouth, it is a problem or whenever you show up at a gathering, it seems like things go wrong. At one point in my life, I had that experience that seemed like my mere presence, or the sound of my voice caused others to be uncomfortable. I could not understand what and why this was happening. Joseph's presence caused his brothers to feel so uncomfortable to the point where they plotted to get rid of him by trying to kill him.

"When Joseph's brothers saw him coming, they recognized him in the distance. As he approached, they made plans to kill him. Here comes the dreamer!" they said. "Come on, let's kill him and throw him into one of these cisterns..." **Genesis 37:18-20 (NLT)**

Our dreams and our visions are easily killed by others. Each day, we must seek God's guidance for our lives. God's grace and favor engulf us, and other see the anointing of God on our lives, and that can either causes them to respect it and embrace us or reject us and want to kill us. When our dreams and visions are exposed to our enemies, and it is a threat to them, then they would in turn, want to kill us. We look at things concerning our lives too passively and that opens the door for our enemies to creep in and create turmoil. But remember, when God favors you and His anointing is over your live, no one can stop your dream. That spotlight is over you;

you are walking under an open heaven, and the trusted enemies that you call friends, brothers, and sisters cannot stand that glare over your life and would do everything to out or dim your light. That dream, that vision you had, the enemy does not want your vision to be fulfilled because your vision threatens your enemies. They somehow can see the outcome of your dream and will try their utmost best to stop it. But do not get distracted by the enemy's plan; they will throw things to distract you to get you off your path, keeping you from achieving your purpose; do not let that distract you. They will put negative thoughts about your ideas, dreams, and visions to discourage others from your vision. Even though that was the same vision that friend and her husband supported you to fulfill. That lunch I had was my best friend and her husband who set it up; she was with me, supporting and giving me ideas, but still, it was not a good idea. I felt so crushed; my hope was gone, and it was all because of another person's emotions. Their feeling towards my success, a success a friend needed to embrace. As children of God, we must be discerning enough to discern the scheme of the enemy, as Ephesians says.

"Put on the whole armour of God, that ye may be able to stand against the wiles of the devil." **Ephesians 6:11 (KJV)**

"So, when Joseph came to his brothers, they stripped him of his robe, the robe of many colors that he wore. And they took him and threw him into a pit. The pit was empty; there was no water in it." **Genesis 37:23-24 (ESV)**

You may be stripped of your colorful robe, you experienced that divorce, you lost that loved one, that dream job is no longer a dream, or the betrayal from your friends left you feeling as though you are in a pit like Joseph being thrown into a pit, but guess what, yes you were in a pit all of the trials you faced, that pit was dry as there was no water in your pit to overtake you, so consider it your dry season. The enemy's main purpose was to keep you in that pit where you battle with that depression and betrayal; they thought you wouldn't make it because you were in that pit. As a matter of fact, they know the pit would take you out, but they didn't know God's hand was upon you; he was with you through it all; He didn't leave you alone. His grace and the anointing upon your life cause you to survive that dry season in the pit. Looking at it, that pit didn't hold you back; the enemy's plan turned into your Favor. You remained faithful to his words; you kept praising him; you remained in the church; it didn't bother you; you continued serving in your ministry. You find joy in the pit; you'll regain your strength in that pit; consider it a holding place until God is ready to elevate you. And you will be elevated. Don't listen to the negative words from people; stay focused on Him. When others who are not happy for you see your elevation, they will talk but remember they are talking to look good in the eyes of others. God will get you out, I was in the pit and I was able to come out of it. Looking at what I have achieved, and I did it while in the pit, I know it was only God. Stay focused, don't look at it as a pit, it's your holding season, your recouping season. A season for you to reflect upon your life.

My sisters, as you ponder upon your life's experiences or your pit experiences, do not take it to heart where you would let go of the hurt or pain caused by others. For us to move ahead in life, we must have a forgiving heart. Forgive those who have done us wrong; when we forgive, we will experience the liberty to worship the Lord. We must acknowledge that what you went through was a process of 'the pit experiences,' and yes, it was an experience because I am sure you have learned from those experiences. You survived this experience; there are some people who could not make it through their pit experiences; they lost their minds, and the emotional trauma was too severe. But because of the promises of God and the anointing on your life, you made it through; here you are, you are still standing. It does not matter what you went through; just look at your surroundings and lift your eyes, you'll see that you are not in a pit; where you are right now is not a pit environment; you were in a pit but not in it. You see my sisters, when

Joesph was in Egypt; it was a pit because he was not in his homeland with his father and brothers, but he was serving in his Egyptian master's home in charge of his Egyptian master's household and property while in that pit. So, I am encouraging you to rise from your pit, and go follow your dream!

"When Joseph was taken to Egypt by the Ishmaelite traders, he was purchased by Potiphar, an Egyptian officer. Potiphar was captain of the guard for Pharaoh, the king of Egypt. The Lord was with Joseph, so he succeeded in everything he did as he served in the home of his Egyptian master. Potiphar noticed this and realized that the Lord was with Joseph, giving him success in everything he did. This pleased Potiphar, so he soon made Joseph his personal attendant. He put him in charge of his entire household and everything he owned."

Genesis 39:1-4 (NLT)

Notes

West, B., 2019, A Colorful Impact: The Psychological Impact of Colors

www.jofsr.org

Genesis 34:3-4 (KJV), Rights in the Authorized (King James) Version in the United Kingdom are vested in the Crown. Published by permission of the Crown's patentee, Cambridge University Press.

Genesis 37:9-10 (NLT), Holy Bible, New Living Translation copyright 1996, 2004, 2007, 2015 by Tyndale House Foundation

Genesis 37:23-24 (ESV), The Holy Bible, English Standard Version (ESV). copyright ©2001 by Crossway, a publishing ministry of Good News Publishers

Genesis 37:18-20 (NLT), Holy Bible, New Living Translation copyright 1996, 2004, 2007, 2015 by Tyndale House Foundation

Acknowledgements

I can truly say that as we go along life's journey, God places people in our life that will motivate and inspire us to attain that purpose in life. I would like to extend my gratitude to those who played a significant part in this accomplishment. First and foremost, I would like to give thanks to God, the head of my life. Lord, I couldn't have made it without you. As I looked over my life, you have truly been a blessing to me. Thank you.

Dr. Kishma George, thank you for always being there with your creative ideas; they have really inspired me. God bless you.

To my spiritual family, thank you all for your love.

To my son Uri, thank you for your encouragement. I love you son.

To my niece Kaylee G., you are my supporter. Aunty loves you.

Finally, to all my friends, I love you all.

Dr. Sharon O. Simon

Sharon O. Simon is a servant in the Kingdom, was born and raised in Georgetown, Guyana, South America. She is the last child in a family of six and has two brothers and three sisters. Her family migrated to the United States in 1991 to pursue a better life and to be a part of the American dream. At the age of 31, she was able to achieve her then-driven goal of becoming a mother and a homeowner. In 2003, after facing some challenges in life, she decided to follow the path that God has for her life. As an Administrator, her mission is to use her spiritual gift in the kingdom to help religious organizations/ministries cultivate an environment that eliminates any pressure points as they evolve.

Sharon O. Williams-Simon holds a Bachelor of Professional Studies in Health Services Administration, an Advanced Certificate in Public Health, and a Doctorate Degree in Theology. She is now seeking this new call of authorship or being an author. She believes that everyone in the kingdom is peculiar and has something unique to offer. Her desire is to see servants of God remain steadfast and persevere towards their mark in spite of the circumstances. When she is not actively involved in the ministry, Sharon loves spending her leisure time traveling with her family. Dr. Sharon O. resides in New York with her son, Uri.

Contact information.

Website:
www.sharonoslynsimon.com
Facebook:
www.facebook.com/SharonO.Simon
Email:
Drsharono@sharonosimon.com
Phone:
718-216-0465

Books by Dr.Kishma published by ChosenButterfly Publishing

All Books are available on Amazon, Kindle and wherever books are sold online

| When New Life Begins | Bringing Forth the Dreamer in You | Dreaming the Dream | The Princess in You | Dreamer on the Rise |

    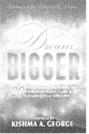

| Awaken the Dreamer | Birthing the Dreamer in You | From a Doubter to a Dreamer | Use What's In Your Hand | Dream Bigger |

When You Have a Dream · The Power of Vision · Dreamer in You · Gleaming Dreamers (A children's book) *Published by Kishma. A George Enterprise*

Made in the USA
Coppell, TX
07 December 2023